101 KEY IDEAS

Business Studies

Neil Denby

TEACH YOURSELF BOOKS

For UK order queries: please contact Bookpoint Ltd, 130 Milton Park, Abingdon, Oxon OX14 4SB. Telephone: (44) 01235 827720. Fax: (44) 01235 400454. Lines are open from 9.00–18.00, Monday to Saturday, with a 24-hour message answering service. Email address: orders@bookpoint.co.uk

For USA order queries: please contact McGraw-Hill Customer Services, P.O. Box 545, Blacklick, OH 43004-0545, USA. Telephone: 1-800-722-4726. Fax: 1-614-755-5645.

For Canada order queries: please contact McGraw-Hill Ryerson Ltd., 300 Water St, Whitby, Ontario L1N 9B6, Canada. Telephone: 905 430 5000. Fax: 905 430 5020.

Long-renowned as the authoritative source for self-guided learning – with more than 30 million copies sold worldwide – the *Teach Yourself* series includes over 300 titles in the fields of languages, crafts, hobbies, business and education.

British Library Cataloguing in Publication Data
A catalogue entry for this title is available from The British Library.

Library of Congress Catalog Card Number: on file

First published in UK 2001 by Hodder Headline Plc, 338 Euston Road, London NW1 3BH.

First published in US 2001 by Contemporary Books, a division of the McGraw-Hill Companies, 4255 West Touhy Avenue, Lincolnwood (Chicago), Illinois 60712–1975, USA.

The 'Teach Yourself' name and logo are registered trade marks of Hodder & Stoughton Ltd.

Copyright © 2001 Neil Denby

Cover illustration by Mike Stones.
Typeset by Transet Limited, Coventry, England.
Printed in Great Britain for Hodder & Stoughton Educational, a division of Hodder Headline Plc, 338 Euston Road, London NW1 3BH by Cox & Wyman Ltd, Reading, Berkshire.

Impression number	10 9 8 7 6 5 4 3 2 1
Year	2007 2006 2005 2004 2003 2002 2001

Contents

Introduction

Welcome to the **Teach Yourself 101 Key Ideas** series. We hope that you will find both this book and others in the series to be useful, interesting and informative. The purpose of the series is to provide an introduction to a wide range of subjects, in a way that is entertaining and easy to absorb.

Each book contains 101 short accounts of key ideas or terms which are regarded as central to that subject. The accounts are presented in alphabetical order for ease of reference. All of the books in the series are written in order to be meaningful whether or not you have previous knowledge of the subject. They will be useful to you whether you are a general reader, are on a pre-university course, or have just started at university.

We have designed the series to be a combination of a text book and a dictionary. We felt that many text books are too long for easy reference, while the entries in dictionaries are often too short to provide sufficient

detail. The **Teach Yourself 101 Key Ideas** series gives the best of both worlds! Here are books that you do not have to read cover to cover, or in any set order. Dip into them when you need to know the meaning of a term, and you will find a short, but comprehensive account which will be of real help with those essays and assignments. The terms are described in a straightforward way with a careful selection of academic words thrown in for good measure!

So if you need a quick and inexpensive introduction to a subject, **Teach Yourself 101 Key Ideas** is for you. And incidentally, if you have any suggestions about this book or the series, do let us know. It would be great to hear from you.

Best wishes with your studies!

Paul Oliver
Series Editor

ACAS

The Advisory, Conciliation and Arbitration Service was established by the government in 1975 as an independent body. Its job is to provide an independent service of advice and negotiation in industrial disputes. When there is an unresolved dispute, i.e. a breakdown in industrial relations between employer and employees, ACAS will step in, on request, to try to solve the problem. It also provides free information and advice. The four main functions of ACAS are linked to its title:

Advice – ACAS will advise both employers and employee groups in an attempt to prevent industrial disputes from arising; it will also provide information and encourage better industrial relations, having established a number of free information centres. It will provide guidance for employers and employees on best practice and on other issues such as training.

Conciliation – ACAS will, on request, work with both sides to solve industrial disputes if they do happen.

Arbitration and mediation – If conciliation does not work, ACAS can provide an independent mediator or arbitrator. A mediator will try to bring both sides closer together when negotiations have broken down, s/he can propose a solution to the dispute, but neither side is obliged to accept it. If this fails, or as an alternative to mediation, an arbitrator can be called in by either side. The arbitrator will weigh the arguments on both sides of the dispute and propose a solution. Neither side is obliged to accept this decision. However, often both sides agree to accept the result of the arbitration before it is made. This can then be made legally binding on both parties. This is a reflection of the confidence which both employers and employee groups place in ACAS. It is a body which is trusted to be independent in its judgement.

> ### see also...
> *Government policies; Industrial relations*

AIDA

Promotion involves communicating the existence, features and benefits of a product to a consumer or potential consumer. The intention is to do one of three things:

- increase or create consumer awareness of products
- encourage consumers to remember a product
- persuade consumers to buy the product.

The main method of achieving these aims is through advertising. The AIDA acronym is used to remember the qualities that advertising should possess. It should attract Attention; create Interest; develop Desire and lead to Action.

Ways of *attracting attention* include the use of the various advertising media. Media are priced according to their effectiveness and reach – the number of potential customers who will see the advertisement. The most effective in terms of reaching large numbers – and therefore the most expensive – is the use of television broadcast media. Broadcast media also includes commercial radio. Radio advertisements will reach a wide audience and can be more effective than television advertising. Other mass media include national newspapers and magazines. These have the advantage of targeting particular market segments. Newspapers will only be aimed at particular socio-economic groups while magazines tend to be targeted even more precisely at different market segments such as hobbies and interests, gender and age.

Creating interest in a product is important if advertisers are going to move on to the third and fourth parts – *desire* and *action*. Often advertisements will extol some of the virtues of a product without actually mentioning its price – a ploy designed to get consumers to enquire after the product themselves. If advertisers can convince the consumer that the product is something that they need, or will derive pleasure or use from, then the desire has been created and the action – of buying the product – should follow.

see also...

Promotion; Branding Market segmentation

Aims and objectives of business

Businesses all have targets, or objectives, that they are trying to reach. Some may be very long-term objectives that are going to be difficult to ever realize. These are often stated as 'mission statements'. The Coca Cola company, for example, states that it wishes to become 'the beverage of choice' – i.e. to replace tea, coffee and even water as the chosen drink of people! Some objectives are seen as stepping stones on the way to the wider objective – these may be called targets, or intermediate objectives.

Business objectives can, broadly speaking, be put into three categories: satisficing objectives, maximizing objectives and minimizing objectives. *Satisficing objectives* are those where a business says: 'I have reached a particular point'; 'I am satisfied'. Satisficing objectives may include survival, breaking even, reaching a certain level of sales or making a certain level of income.

Maximizing objectives are those where a business wants to reach the maximum – the most – of something. Many commentators have made the assumption that all businesses are profit maximizers. There are however, a number of other areas that a business might prefer to maximize such as sales or productivity.

Minimizing objectives are those where a business wants to make the least, rather than the most, of something. A firm might, for example, want to minimize labour turnover due to the expense of appointing and training new workers.

Objectives are often set so that they are SMART targets. This stands for:
- Specific – objectives should be as definite as possible
- Measurable – a target should be quantifiable
- Attainable – a target should be possible to achieve
- Relevant – a target should form a logical part of the business's overall strategy
- Time-related – there should be a time set for achievement.

see also...

Business plans; Small businesses; Break even

Ansoff matrix

gor Ansoff (an American business writer) devised a matrix to help businesses to see in what directions they might best grow.

lowest risk		A Existing products	B New products	
1	Existing markets	market penetration – low risk, low reward	product development – medium risk, medium reward	
2	New markets	market development – medium risk, medium reward	diversification – high risk, high rewards	highest risk

The lowest risk strategies are at A1, the highest risk at B2. A1, market penetration, is expansion by gaining a foothold in an existing market. To do this the business must be prepared to compete with other businesses which are already established. The strategy carries the lowest levels of risk but also the lowest levels of possible reward.

At A2 the business uses an existing product in order to enter a new market. This could involve repositioning an existing successful product. For example, if rap music could be successfully repositioned so that it appealed to the older age group, this would be a successful expansion (more sales) without having to develop a new product.

At B1 the business is growing by developing new products to sell within its existing markets. This usually involves heavy advertising expenditure and carries a high risk of failure. Success, however, can lead to high rewards. One of the difficulties with this strategy is to come up with a product that does not cannibalize the existing market. Successful expansion has not taken place if consumers merely switch from one product produced by the business to another.

B2 is the highest risk strategy. This involves the introduction of completely new products into completely new markets. This is called *diversification* and can either lead to high levels of success or spectacular failure.

see also...

Management theorists

Appraisal

Appraisal is where one person in a business looks at the way that a worker is doing his/her job and finds out what it is about it that s/he likes, dislikes or does particularly well or badly and where improvements can be made. Appraisal is part of the performance management strategy of a business. Appraisal systems assess the effectiveness of a worker, set *targets* and then evaluate performance against these targets.

Businesses can use formal or informal appraisal systems both to monitor and manage the progress and efficiency of the workforce. In 360 degree appraisal, each person in an organization is appraised by another, including senior managers, directors and the workforce.

The appraisal process usually consists of three phases. Firstly there is the preparation for the appraisal, when the worker and the appraiser collect information (which should include the record of the previous appraisal) and can each highlight any problems or particular areas for discussion. Second is the appraisal interview; this is usually conducted in a fairly informal manner but within a formal framework. Thirdly, there is the continuous monitoring of performance that takes place throughout the year.

The purpose of the appraisal process is to review progress, address problems, suggest solutions and to set objectives for future performance. These objectives need to be linked to SMART targets. The appraisal aims to improve the performance of a worker, provide feedback on current performance and set targets for the future. Appraisal will also highlight training needs and be used to show who is ready for promotion or career enhancement.

The main types of appraisal are:
- Management reviews
- Peer reviews
- Self review.

see also...

Aims and objectives of business

Balance of payments

The balance of payments measures the flows of money into and out of a country. It is linked to the amount of goods and services that are traded by one country with all other countries with which it does business. *Visibles* are products that can actually be seen and handled – cars, textiles, coal and commodities such as coffee and wheat. *Invisibles* are those things that cannot be seen or handled such as tourism, banking and insurance.

The balance of payments shows whether a country is earning more from *sales* of visibles and invisibles abroad than it is paying for *imports* of visibles and invisibles. If the country is paying more out (i.e. importing a greater value of goods and services than the value of its exports) then it is said to have a *deficit* on balance of payments. If it is earning more from exports than it is paying for imports then it has a balance of payments *surplus*. Note that it is the value of the imports and exports that is important rather than any other measurement.

The balance of payments is split into two parts: the *current account*

measures payments for actual goods and services transacted; the *capital account* measures flows of money such as savings and investment. When balance of payments surpluses and deficits are talked about, this will usually refer to the current account balance.

Because it is the value of goods and services which is important, rather than the volume, the balance of payments is affected by changes in exchange rates. If sterling is strong and its value in terms of other currencies is rising, then UK exports become relatively more expensive and imports relatively cheaper.

For a business which imports or exports, the strength or otherwise of a currency will be important. A business which exports most of its production will be happy with a weak currency, as this means that it is earning more abroad; a business which has to import (for example components, raw materials or commodities) a strong currency is better.

see also...

International trade

Balance sheet

The balance sheet is a 'snapshot' – a position at a point in time – of the financial position of a firm. It shows the assets and liabilities of the business. Assets are what the business owns, liabilities are what the business owes. A typical balance sheet could be laid out as follows:

of a business is considered to be its current assets minus its current liabilities. It represents the finance available for the day-to-day operations of the business. Current liabilities – these are amounts that must be paid within 12 months which could include tax liabilities and dividends

Fixed assets	Long-term liabilities		
1 Buildings and land	10 Share capital		
2 Vehicles, equipment, tools,	11 Retain profit		
3 Furniture and fittings	12 Bank loans		
SUB TOTAL of 1, 2, 3.			
Current assets			
4 Stock			
5 Debtors			
6 Cash			
SUB TOTAL of 4, 5, 6			
TOTAL of 1, 2, 3, 4, 5, 6			
Current liabilities			
7 Creditors			
8 Bank overdrafts			
9 Tax liabilities and dividend			
SUB TOTAL of 7, 8, 9			
Net current assets (SUB TOTAL of 4, 5, 6 minus SUB TOTAL of 7, 8, 9)			
Net assets employed (fixed assets plus net current assets)	Capital employed (total of 10, 11, 12). This will equal net assets employed. The balance sheet must balance.		

Fixed assets – these include buildings, plant and machinery, financial assets such as the ownership of shares in other firms and intangible assets such as a brand image or a firm's 'goodwill'.

Current assets – these include material assets and financial assets. Net current assets are also known as working capital. The working capital

Long-term liabilities – these do not have to be paid for at least 12 months and could include items such as mortgages and bank loans. Shareholders' funds comprise issued shares and reserves.

see also...

Cash flow forecast; Costs; Profit and loss account

Blake Mouton grid

There are numerous different styles of management within a business. Each style demonstrates the way in which a particular manager could or would handle a particular situation. If a manager wants a job doing then s/he has to decide what is the best way to get the job done. Some managers are extremely concerned with the job itself, i.e. with production, others might be so concerned with the workers' welfare that the production task becomes secondary and may not even be satisfactorily completed.

The Blake Mouton grid was devised to make the comparison between those managers who are more concerned with people than production and those more concerned with production than people.

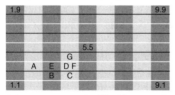

1.1 – unconcerned with either people or production, an 'impoverished' management style.
1.9 – very concerned with workers' welfare, possibly to the detriment of the production task – termed 'country club management'.
5.5 – balancing the concern for people with an equal concern for the task 'middle of the road' management.
9.1 – very concerned with the production task, possibly to the detriment of the workers' welfare.
9.9 – extremely concerned with both people and production – a teamwork approach to management.

All other 'squares' on the grid are also possible.

The grid plots a manager's concern for workers against his or her concern for production. It can be used by a business to identify and modify management styles. For example, a business that found its management styles were clustered as shown (managers A-F) could identify that it was being overly concerned with production to the detriment of its workers (it may, for example, have noted high levels of staff turnover) and take measures to attempt to change its style.

see also...

Management theorists

Boston matrix

The Boston matrix is used to examine the position of each of a business's products in its product portfolio. It allows a business to see which products are achieving their potential and which may need to be supported or divested. Products fall into one of four categories called stars, problem children, cash cows or dogs.

Stars have a high market share in a fast-growing market – they may have been first into a new market (called a blue sky market) and will need high marketing expenditure to keep them competitive as new entrants come into the market. A has achieved a larger turnover than B but has a lower market share in a faster growing market. *Problem children* (C) may also be known as *question marks*. These products have a small market share of a fast-growing market and could provide high future profits – the competitors that are trying to gain a foothold in a blue sky market, competing with products like B, may well be problem children.

Cash cows have a large market share of a mature or slow-growing market. These are established product lines which need little marketing expenditure – often they are market leaders – and which produce cash that can be used to support other products. Product D has a large turnover in a market that is still growing. Product E is a market leader in a market with little growth potential. *Dogs* are products with a small share of a slow-growing market. Product F has a low market share of a market with low growth potential.

Marketing managers can choose whether to keep or lose each product (hold or divest) most usual tactics will be to:
- keep the cows, using the cash to support other products (milking the cows)
- hold the stars – turn the stars into cash cows
- build the problem children – try to turn the problem into stars
- divest the dogs – try to get rid of poorly performing products.

see also...

Product life cycle; Market planning

Brand names and images

A brand is a distinctive name or style that is applied to a product or to a range of products so that it is easily identifiable by the consumer. The brand name may be the name of the business which produces the product (such as the Heinz range of foods or Dyson vacuum cleaners and washing machines) or a name that has been devised and is owned by the business – for example, Barbie is a brand of Mattel. A successful brand name will be linked to a brand image.

A brand image is more than just a brand name. A marketing department will decide on a particular image according to the target market for the brand. All aspects of the brand will then be developed to reinforce this image. This includes packaging, lettering, slogans, advertising and promotion all working together to build a brand image. A brand leader is the brand with the highest percentage share of a particular market. This is a powerful position for a product to be in as many major retailers will only stock brand leaders and their own branded products.

Businesses develop and maintain brands so that customers will be loyal to their products and choose the branded product ahead of the competition. This may be because the customer has enjoyed a good experience with another product with the same brand name or because the establishment of a brand image has been successful and the customer associates the brand with something in particular (such as quality, value for money, reliability). Brand loyalty, once established, is very difficult to shift and can be a major obstacle to new products entering an established market. Branded goods are usually more expensive than the equivalent unbranded product due to the amount of money that has to be spent on promoting and supporting the brand.

Brand names are very important to many businesses and are often included in the business's assets. They are so important that they are registered and protected by law. Anyone copying, faking or impersonating a brand is liable to prosecution.

see also...

AIDA; Promotion

Break even

This is the financial position where the total revenue of a business (the total amount of money coming into the business from sales and other activities) is equal to the total cost. At this point the business is making neither a profit nor a loss. It can be shown on a break-even chart which is made up of four lines: fixed costs, variable costs, total costs and sales revenue.

Fixed costs are those which do not alter as output alters, this is therefore shown on the graph as a horizontal line (FC). *Variable costs* are those that vary as output varies and are therefore shown as rising as output rises (VC). Adding fixed costs to variable costs gives *total costs* (TC). The addition of total *revenue from sales* completes the graph (TR). The point where total cost is equal to total revenue is the break-even point. To the left of this point, total costs are higher than total revenue, so the business is making a loss; to the right of this point, total costs are lower than total revenue, so the business is making a profit. The further away sales are from the break-even point, the greater the profit or loss.

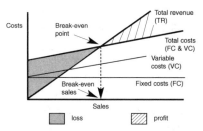

The contribution method of working out the break-even point does away with the graph and instead looks at the *contribution* of each sale to overall revenue. Contribution is calculated by taking the variable cost of the product away from its fixed cost. The formula is

> break-even sales = fixed costs/contribution

Note that there is a difference between break-even output (as the break-even point is often quoted) and break-even sales. Break-even output is easier to reach than break-even sales as all output is not necessarily sold.

---

see also...

Costs; Sources of finance;

Business growth

Expansion of a business will be within the terms which that business uses for its own measurement of size – a small firm in a small market may double in size and double its market share but still be nowhere near as big as a small firm in a large market. Businesses that wish to expand will do it through either internal growth or external growth.

In *internal growth* the business expands without involving other businesses in mergers or take-overs. Internal growth may be achieved through the introduction of new products or through what is termed 'organic' growth, growth from within the business. Internal growth tends to be slower than external but has the advantage of not involving anyone from outside of the organization. While the growth may be gradual it will also be less traumatic and possibly more permanent.

Organic growth involves a business growing from within by ploughing back its own profits into growth. The business may use these funds to take on more employees, open new outlets or open new plants. The business will concentrate on increasing the sales of its core product or products rather than expanding into any new products or markets. In some cases this may be a case of using product extension strategies to lengthen the life of a product but businesses can be extremely successful at this.

External growth is achieved through either acquisition or integration. This is buying into, joining together with or taking over another company. Sometimes this is with the consent of the other business – usually termed a merger, sometimes without its consent, in which case it is termed a hostile take-over. Integration can take place in several directions, depending on the relative positions in the chain of production of the businesses involved.

see also...

Product life cycle

Business plans

The business plan is an outline of what aims and objectives the business intends to achieve and the strategies, staff and products it intends to employ to achieve them. It should include details such as cash flow forecasts, break-even forecasts and a business model. It should be based on market research into the business's chosen market and should include all aspects of the business, not just finance but the products for sale, marketing strategy, structure and administration of the business. A good business plan lays down the direction that the business will take and outlines targets and objectives. It is a working document for the business; one to which the owners and staff can and should refer often. It is not just a vehicle to show to a bank manager in order to get a loan but an important management tool that should be updated at regular intervals.

The business plan should be presented to look professional and readable. The main sections of a typical business plan are:

- Cover containing a very brief introduction to the business, carrying the logo and mission statement to give an instant flavour of the business.
- Contents to make navigation easier for the reader.
- A brief history of the business then a summary of the plan which presents an overview.
- Details of the legal format of the business.
- Aims and objectives and how the business intends to reach them.
- Unique Selling Point. This section should compare the product with two or more competitors and say what makes it special and likely to succeed.
- Market information should be drawn from the market research carried out and show what the target market is and how it will be reached.
- Personnel will show the management structure of the business and the skills or expertise of any key staff.
- Finances will show the current financial position of the business and how it intends to raise any further money.
- Any other factors of note

see also...

Break even; Ratios; Profitability

Business press

Often the best way to have a business problem or issue explained is through the pages of the business press. Apart from those publications that are particular to specific professions (such as *Accountancy Age*) there is a wide range of general business publications that can help in understanding the business world. The most widely available are the business sections of national newspapers which will cover items of interest to the 'average' reader. This will include items on both personal finance and business finance such as savings, building societies, stocks and shares, insurance, unit trusts, legal rights, consumer rights and taxation.

Newspaper business sections are targeted, of course, at the intended readership of the newspaper. Thus the business pages in the tabloid press are likely to be written in a more popular style and with less depth and detail than those in the more serious papers. Nevertheless, even such business reports as the tabloids carry can keep you up to date with current developments in the business world – often (in

particular in the more 'upmarket' tabloids) explained in a way which is much more easy to understand.

The main national newspaper concentrating on business and financial news is the *Financial Times*. Although it has a business and financial slant, the newspaper still carries general news and articles and is trying to move away from its image of being just for financial news.

Weekend newspapers are also likely to carry business supplementary sections which offer a number of features ranging from news items, share tips and information, company and individual profiles to explanations of tax positions, new laws and regulations. These can be a vital source of up-to-date and well-explained information which could save a business money in consultation fees with an accountant, lawyer or financial adviser.

see also...

Personalities

Cash flow forecast

This is a prediction of the future flows of cash into and out of a business.

The main cash inflows are the owner's own funds, borrowed funds and revenue from sales and services.

of £50 at the end of the year. The most the business needs to borrow will be £200, and then only for one month (April). Such forecasts can be particularly important for businesses which see seasonal fluctuations in their demand.

Month	Jan	Feb	Mar	Apr	May	Jun	July	Aug	Sept	Oct	Nov	Dec
Cash in bank b/fwd	200	250	150	–50	–200	100	50	50	–50	100	50	0
Sales revenue	400	400	300	200	600	250	300	150	400	300	300	400
TOTAL CASH	600	650	450	150	400	350	350	200	350	400	350	400
Interest	50	50	50	50	50	50	50	50	50	50	50	50
Rent	50	50	50	50	50	50	50	50	50	50	50	50
Stock	150	300	300	150	100	100	100	50	50	150	150	150
Other	100	100	100	100	100	100	100	100	100	100	100	100
TOTAL CASH OUT	350	500	500	350	300	300	300	250	250	350	350	350
Bank balance c/fwd	250	150	–50	–200	100	50	50	–50	100	50	0	50

The main outflows are purchase of stock, running expenses, interest payments, taxation and the distribution of profits. If there is more flowing into a business than leaving it the business has a cash surplus; if there is more flowing out than in, there is a cash deficit. The cash flow forecast is a month-by-month prediction of how much cash will be needed, which can then be compared with what was actually needed. The figure below represents a typical cash flow forecast for a full year. The business has a cash surplus of £200 at the start of the year and a surplus

The forecast can also be shown on a bar chart.

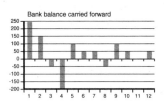

Bank balance carried forward

A shortage of cash, rather than a lack of orders, is the reason for the failure of many businesses.

see also...

Balance sheet; Profit and loss account; Costs; Break even

Cell production

Cell production is a development that has taken place as part of the move towards lean production techniques. The just-in-time method that is at the heart of lean production needs both flexible machinery and flexible working practices in order to work efficiently. Lean production techniques have therefore led to an enhanced form of personnel management called Human Resources Management (HRM), a 'person-centred' system of managing people sometimes referred to as lean person management.

HRM encourages a business to look at all aspects of its human resources and is particularly concerned in keeping them satisfied and motivated. Studies (notably Elton Mayo's Relay Assembly Test at the Hawthorne plant in Chicago between 1927 and 1932) found that workers increased productivity and motivation if they worked as a team, with good communications and management showing an interest in their progress. The use of cell production is a method of encouraging team work and a team ethos. Motivation studies have shown that this is important for efficiency. Instead of working on a production line, repeating the same task, workers work in small teams. Teams work in separate bays or cells, each producing a component or completing a particular process. This is then passed on to the next part of the process. This approach involves job enlargement and job enrichment, gives each team greater responsibility and encourages competition between teams. Such team working also encourages a culture of 'right first time' in that mistakes should either not happen (a culture of prevention rather than cure) or, if they do, should be rectified immediately before being passed down the line.

The problems with the breakdown of such a system are enormous – if no buffer stocks are held then any failure of any part of the production line will lead to the halting of all production. It is, however, in the interests of all teams (including suppliers) to ensure that this does not happen.

see also...

HRM; Lean production

Conditions of demand

These are the background conditions that will affect which products consumers will demand. They are the factors other than price, price of substitutes and complements, income and taste or fashion. Changes in these background factors tend to lead to changes that are slower but generally more far reaching and permanent.

In particular these factors include the population size and structure. The bigger the population, the bigger the potential market. For example, ice cream manufacturers Unilever (Walls brand) are currently part way through a long-term strategy to open up China – a very large potential market – to its ice cream. Population structure will also affect patterns of demand. An ageing population will require more medical care, pensions and home nursing, while demand for 'young' products like pop music and bicycles will fall. Businesses need to look at such trends when planning future product lines or marketing campaigns.

The income distribution of a population is also important; a population may seem to be rich if the total domestic product is divided by the number of the population, but demand patterns will be very different depending on whether the income is distributed evenly throughout the population or whether concentrations of income are held in the hands of the rich. (On the whole, there is an uneven distribution of income in most countries and certainly in the world – the richest 6 per cent in the world own approximately 60 per cent of the world's wealth.) Expenditure patterns for populations will alter as particular levels of disposable income are reached.

Some products have to contend with seasonal variations in demand and need marketing techniques to iron these out. An obvious example is ice cream, where demand will increase as the weather gets hotter.

see also...

Demand; Elasticity of demand

Co-operatives

A co-operative enterprise is one where a group of people have come together to work or to buy or sell goods or services for the mutual benefit of the group (the definition includes mutual societies). The main types of business co-operative are consumer co-ops, worker co-ops and producer co-ops. All work on the same basis of mutual help and shared resources and returns.

The Rochdale Pioneers were the forerunners of the modern consumer co-operative movement. A group of workers in Rochdale, Lancashire, formed the Rochdale Society of Equitable Pioneers in 1844 in order to supply members with fair prices for basic goods. The co-operative retail society (CRS) now has a turnover in excess of £8,000 million and 5,000 retail outlets nationwide.

In 1869 the Co-operative Union was formed. This is a body that helps and advises on the formation of new co-operative enterprises. It now forms an umbrella body under which are the CRS, the Co-operative Wholesale Society and other co-operative enterprises.

Worker co-operatives are where a group of workers decide to share the work, decision making and profits of a business between them.

The major features of worker co-operatives are shared decision making, shared risk and shared profit.

Worker co-operatives have less chance of industrial relations problems, produce better motivation in workers as they are working for themselves and tend to be more aware of responsibilities to the local community where the workers live. On the other hand growth of the organization is difficult and it is harder to raise capital.

Producers co-operatives are a common feature of many societies. In parts of Africa, for example, several villages will join together at harvest time in order to gain mutual benefits. In South America, smaller producers of coffee have joined together to co-operate in the branding and marketing of their own produce.

see also...

Mutual societies and demutualization

Communication

Effective communication is vital to the efficient running of a business. Communications requires four elements: a sender, a medium, a message and a receiver. If any one of these elements does not function properly then the communication is inefficient. Communication can be categorized in a number of ways. It will be internal or external, formal or informal and may be lateral or horizontal. External communication is with organizations outside the business such as suppliers and customers. Internal is within the organization. This internal communication may be between people at the same level of the organization (such as managers) in which case it is termed horizontal communication, or between people at different levels of the organization (such as a manager to a director or a worker) in which case it is termed vertical communication. If a business establishes a team consisting of people from different levels of the organization (such as a project team) to carry out a particular task or function then the communication within this team is termed lateral or matrix communication. Formal channels are those communications which take place within a defined framework and parameters. Examples include interviews, reports and board meetings. Examples of informal channels include conversation and notice boards. Informal channels can sometimes be more efficient at disseminating information than formal ones (and thus more powerful); this is often referred to as 'the grapevine'.

The medium through which a communication is sent may be verbal, written or electronic and the choice of medium will depend on the nature of the message. Does it, for example, need to be kept private or secure or should it be reaching the widest possible audience?

Good communication is seen as a vital part of good business practice. Instructions need to be clear and precise, feedback needs to be distinct, lucid and genuine, information for the rest of the organization needs to be as widely disseminated as necessary.

see also...

Managing change

Competition Commission

Sometimes competition in a market does not operate in the best interests of the consumer. In such cases, the government may find it necessary to intervene. Often this involves the investigation of monopolies, oligopolies and other restrictive practices and the investigation of proposed mergers that might lead to monopolistic situations that could be against the public interest. *Monopolies* are businesses which have such a large share of a market that they can control either price or output in the market; an *oligopoly* is where a small group of businesses control a market. This is usually against the interest of consumers if the oligopolists are able to collude in fixing price or supply, rather than competing with each other. Business may also operate restrictive practices. These are where the business is able to interfere with the normal operation of the market in a way that brings advantages to them and disadvantages to the consumer. Government has intervened by setting up independent bodies to deal with possible problems.

The Office of Fair Trading (OFT), set up in 1973, is empowered to look into the operations of markets and decide whether actions taken are in the public interest or not. It is an advisory body to the government and recommends which businesses or mergers need to be investigated to the Competition Commission.

The Competition Commission was established as the Monopolies and Mergers Commission by the Fair Trading Act in 1973. This took over the job from the Monopolies Commission, which was established in 1948. It is a government-funded body that investigates proposed mergers to see if they are likely to be against the public interest. If the merger would result in a monopoly or other situation against the public interest, the Commission is empowered to refuse permission for it to go ahead. It also has the power to investigate existing monopolies and can recommend that a monopoly is broken up into smaller units.

see also...

Business growth; Integration

Consumer protection

Government intervenes on behalf of consumers by passing legislation to protect them from possible exploitation by businesses. Businesses may indulge in practices that are either deemed to be unfair, illegal or morally reprehensible and laws are passed to prevent this from happening.

The law in the UK regards the first line of consumer defence as the consumer. A consumer is expected to take every reasonable care to make sure that they have bought the right product for the purpose and that they have read, understood and followed any instructions. The Latin tag for this is *caveat emptor* – let the buyer beware – and it is a main principle of consumer law.

The legislation covers the main issues that will be of concern to consumers. The Food and Drugs Act makes it illegal to sell goods that are 'unfit for human consumption' and covers the accurate labelling of produce. The Trades Descriptions Act states that accurate descriptions of goods must be given wherever they are described. The Consumer Credit Act lays down that full information regarding the costs of credit purchases must be clearly given. The Consumer Protection Acts cover issues such as sale prices being genuine and the labelling of potentially harmful or dangerous goods such as paints, electrical goods, solvents and irritants. The Sale of Goods Acts and The Supply of Goods and Services Act say that goods must be of a satisfactory quality to be sold and must fulfil the purpose for which they are sold.

Consumer legislation has a number of effects on businesses. It may increase the costs of the business by requiring certain standards to be maintained, for example of hygiene or packaging. It may persuade the business of the need for a customer care policy or customer care department, a move which many businesses have seen as necessary. It may lead to better quality management systems being implemented in businesses; this could actually have the effect of cutting costs.

see also...

Government policies; Marketing constraints

Corporate culture

Corporate or organizational culture refers to the way in which an organization works, to the ethos of the organization. It refers to the commonly held beliefs and accepted patterns of working within a particular organization. The culture of the business will have a great effect on how it is viewed by consumers, competitors and by its own workers.

The corporate culture will determine the way in which the company operates and how it interacts with both its employees and other companies with which it deals. Corporate culture defines the attitudes, beliefs and values of the organization and is strongly linked to the aims and objectives of the organization.

Corporate culture may be influenced by ethical considerations, where the business wants to be seen to be helping the environment or not taking advantage of weaker organizations or countries. It may be influenced by economic considerations, such as the need to make a profit, and this can lead to a reward-orientated and acquisitive culture which seeks profit and success regardless of the consequences (dubbed by prime minister Edward Heath in 1973 as the 'unpleasant and unacceptable face of capitalism'). It may be influenced by the nature of the business itself – a business within the legal profession may, for example, have a culture which shows stability and establishment, the sort of qualities which a client may well want in a legal service.

The main types of culture are generally recognized as the following:
- Power culture – this is typical of the businesses with an owner manager; all decisions are centralized and made by a single individual, other contributions to decision making are discouraged.
- Role culture – typified by a business with senior managers whose power is due to their function within the organization.
- Task culture – where the overriding imperative is to 'finish the job' and move on to the next job.
- Person culture – which emphasizes and values the people in the organization.

see also...
Branding; Globalization

Cost and profit centres

Cost and profit centres are parts of the tools of management accounting. They are the business or part of a business to which particular costs or profits are allocated. A cost and profit centre can be treated as a 'business within a business'.

The divisions allow managers to compare the performance of one part of the business with another, to see which is performing better; it allows them to see what works best (i.e. 'best practice') and to apply this to other centres if appropriate; it also allows them to keep a closer control over the various parts of the business.

Difficulties arise when managers are trying to allocate costs. Some costs can be allocated directly to a centre (such as the cost of the raw materials used in a manufacturing process at a plant). These are called *direct costs*. Other, indirect, costs cannot be directly allocated to a cost centre. For example, if the company advertized its products nationally, the cost could only be allocated to centres in proportion. One method, called *full costing*, is to allocate such costs in the same proportion as direct costs. Another method is to use *absorption costing*. This method allocates indirect costs as far as possible to the cost centre where they actually occur.

A third method of allocating costs is called *contribution* or *marginal costing*. In this method, fixed costs are not arbitrarily allocated to cost centres, but instead are calculated. The contribution made by each cost centre is calculated as its revenue minus its variable costs. This can also be stated as price minus marginal cost. In this way, the contribution of each cost centre can clearly be seen.

Allocating profits to centres can also prove difficult since, as often happens, more than one plant or part of a company can be involved in the production process. Similar techniques to cost allocation can be used to try to allocate profits to centres.

see also...

Management accounting; Variances

Cost benefit analysis

Cost benefit analysis compares the costs of a proposed enterprise or project – financial and social – with the likely financial and social benefits. Social costs are the internal costs to the business carrying out the project and the external costs borne by the community (such as noise, congestion and pollution). Social benefits are the internal benefits to the business plus any external benefits. These are often referred to as private and public costs and benefits.

The calculation for working out whether there is an overall benefit is: social benefit minus social costs where *social benefit* equals internal benefits (usually revenues to the business) plus external benefits (to the community), and *social costs* equal internal costs (to the business) plus external costs (to the community).

Cost benefit analysis is very hard to achieve accurately as the quantification of many costs and benefits is difficult. For example, if there was a proposal to build a new motorway, it would be easy to quantify financial costs but also necessary to quantify public costs. If the road would take 20 minutes off a journey time, this would be given a money value; if the new road went through less built-up areas, avoiding schools and shopping areas, an estimate would be made of the likely reduction in road accidents and each would be given a monetary value. *Benefits* might also include less noise, cleaner air and a better health record for the people that the road is now avoiding. *Costs*, however, would have to include the trade lost by shops and garages over the old route and any despoliation of views or natural habitat caused by the new road.

Difficulties in measuring costs and benefits has meant that cost benefit analysis has often had a bad press. If an organization particularly wants a project to go ahead, it is easy for it either to ignore or underestimate the external costs or to over-emphasize the external benefits.

> ### see also...
> *Anxiety; World*

Costs (financial)

Businesses need to be able to identify and categorize where various costs are arising so that the health of the business can be calculated. Profit is the difference between total cost and total revenue, so one way to increase profit (or cut losses) is to reduce costs. To be able to do this businesses divide costs into various groups and sub-groups.

Business costs are usually divided into fixed costs, often called indirect costs or overheads, and variable costs. *Fixed costs* are those costs which do not vary with output, such as rent, loan interest repayments, the uniform business rate and insurance payments. They are those costs which have to be paid whether or not a business produces a product. *Variable costs* are those costs that do vary with output, such as raw materials, packaging, parts and components, ingredients, power and labour charges. *Total cost* is fixed cost plus variable cost.

Sometimes it is difficult to decide whether a cost is fixed or variable as it may have elements of both within it. A power or telecommunications bill, for example, will have a fixed element for the supply of the service, plus a variable element for the amount of the service used. There are also *semi-variable costs* – these are costs that vary with output, but do not do so directly.

Average costs are important to a business as they show the optimum output of the firm, i.e. the point at which it is operating most efficiently. Average costs are total cost divided by total output.

Marginal cost is the cost of producing one extra item. A business maximizes profit where marginal cost equals marginal revenue.

Costs may also be divided into start-up costs and running costs. *Start-up costs* are only paid initially, when setting up a business (such as initial stock, premises and machinery) but repayments for such costs are likely to become part of the fixed costs of a business. *Running costs* are those which have to be paid to keep the business operational. These may be fixed costs such as rent, or variable costs such as wages.

see also...
Break even; Small businesses

Critical path analysis

Project planning is a major part of controlling operations and includes the technique of critical path analysis. This technique breaks a project down into its constituent parts, puts them in the correct sequence and lets managers know when they can plan both to start and complete parts of and whole projects.

Networks are used to show what tasks need to be done, the order of the tasks and the time taken for each task. A node is drawn as a divided circle to show the number of the operation, with the earliest start time for that operation above and the latest finish time below (EST and LFT). Arrows are used to show an activity taking place. The earliest start time for an activity may depend on the activities that have gone before. The latest finish time is the latest that this activity can be finished if it is not to interfere with other activities. Where EST and LFT are not equal, there is 'float time', in effect spare time for that part of the project to be completed. Exceptional operations are those with zero float time.

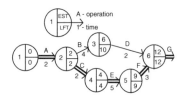

In the figure A is the first activity, it takes two days to complete. B and C are both dependent on A: B takes four days, C takes two days. D cannot be started until B has finished. E is dependent on C, and F on E. G depends on the completion of D and F (perhaps two parts being put together). The critical path is shown by the double lines. There is float time for activities B and D (a total of six days required for completion) as activities C, E and F will take a total of ten days to complete. Networks can be used for planning and to give an overview of a project; the biggest problem with networks is that they can grow so big and complex as to be meaningless.

see also...

Market planning; Operations management

Decision making

usiness decisions are made by the managers of businesses: in some cases this will be the owner; in other cases it will be professional management appointed specifically to take decisions. It is an essential part of the management cycle which begins with target setting (a decision) and continues on to devising strategy, communicating strategy, organizing teams and resources, delegating responsibility, monitoring, motivating and reporting. All of this co-ordination and control requires decisions to be made.

The types of decisions made in businesses fall into three categories: operational, tactical and strategic. The highest level of decision making is strategic decisions. These are made by senior managers, such as the directors of a large company. *Strategic decisions* involve the 'big picture' and the long-term future of the business. They are decisions that affect the direction or values of the business. In smaller businesses, decisions such as whether to opt for incorporation and limited liability status, or whether to take on a new partner, can be regarded as strategic decisions because of the effect that they have on the business.

Tactical decisions are made at the next level of management down. These are medium-term decisions taken by middle managers. In general, they are concerned with making the best use of resources to meet targets which have been set at a higher level.

Operational decisions are those that need to be made for the day-to-day running of the business.

Scientific decision making is one technique used to help managers. It breaks the decision-making process into five parts:
- target setting
- data collection
- theorizing and hypothesizing
- testing and
- reviewing.

The technique takes the guesswork out of decision making but, in so doing, removes any openings for flair or innovatory methods.

see also...

Cost benefit analysis

Demand

Businesses produce products. Consumers want products. When those wants are backed up by the means to pay for them, then they are called demand. It is important for a business to know the factors which influence its demand so that it can try to manipulate them to ensure that its products are demanded. The technical study of demand is probably best left to economists, but businesses need to know the basics.

The major influences on demand are what make up the demand function. Demand is a function of price, the price of other goods (substitutes and complements), income and taste or fashion. This is sometimes written as

$$D = f(P, P1\text{-}n, Y, t)$$

where P1-n represents the prices of all other goods, Y represents income and t represents taste or fashion.

Consumers will have a particular price range into which products will fall. They will have an idea of what they think is a 'reasonable' price for a good or service. They have an idea of what marketers call 'vfm' – value for money.

Income levels will determine how much a particular population or market will be prepared to spend on a product. The level of income that is important is disposable income – the net income that is left for expenditure once deductions have been taken off.

Taste or fashion is an important variable that also includes attitudes and trends. It is one of the major ways in which businesses try to attract consumers. Current trends that marketers might identify include the move towards more environmentally friendly products; and the move towards more productive use of leisure time.

Consumers will also look at the comparative prices of other products before deciding whether to buy. Other products include both substitutes (products that are bought instead of others) and complements (products that are bought to go with others).

> ### see also...
> *Elasticity of demand; Conditions of demand*

Distribution strategies

The marketing mix consists of four elements – price, product, promotion and place. 'Place' refers to the premises or other outlets where a product may be sold and to distribution channels – the way that a product may be delivered either to such outlets or to the final consumer. The traditional distribution strategy was via 'long channel' distribution. The chain of distribution was as follows:

producer > manufacturer > wholesaler > retailer > consumer

The problem with such a channel is in the time it takes for a product to traverse it and in the additional expense incurred through the use of so many intermediaries. An intermediary is anyone, such as a merchant, broker or agent, who provides a service to the people before and after them in the chain (a wholesaler, for example, buys in bulk, provides storage and then breaks bulk for the retailer). Shorter channels can be achieved by cutting out elements of this chain. Distribution channels will be chosen by a business according to the most important factors affecting the product. Is it, for example, perishable, fragile, volatile, large or valuable? The shortest channel is called direct supply. This is when the consumer buys direct from the producer.

Distribution strategies that use intermediaries are either push strategies or pull strategies. A *push strategy* involves producers or manufacturers providing incentives and benefits to intermediaries to take items from them. They use such incentives to push the product down the chain of distribution. Any intermediary in the chain can use such strategies: a wholesaler, for example, might offer extra discount to retailers who bought a large enough amount, or regularly enough. *Pull strategies* involve special offers, promotions and so on aimed at the consumer. If the consumer buys the product, this effectively pulls more products through the chain of distribution.

Distribution also includes the outlets where products are sold.

see also...

Marketing mix; Branding

E-commerce

E-commerce and e-business do not mean quite the same thing. *E-business* is used to refer to any business transaction carried out electronically. A word-processed document or the use of e-mail are considered parts of e-business. *E-commerce*, on the other hand, specifically involves procurement, money and the idea of commercial interchange – the relationship between supplier and consumer, buying and selling. E-commerce therefore usually refers to transactions that take place over the internet (world wide web) and is generally thought of as involving a web site – a place on the web where a potential buyer can browse products and then buy remotely for home delivery. It is a rapidly growing marketplace. Recent figures show that the number of users on the internet has grown from three million in 1997, mainly in the United States, to a total of over 100 million worldwide.

For the small- and medium-sized business there are two main possibilities for expansion on the internet. These are B2C and B2B – business to consumer and business to business (with a third, growing market in business to government or B2G as government services in the UK are privatized or put out to tender).

There are two distinct and different routes into business on the internet. The first strategy is to set up as a pure 'dot com' company (the dot com refers to the suffix that identifies the business as an internet company). This means coming up with a sound idea (that no one else has yet tried successfully) and launching yourself onto the internet. This usually means that the business will need commercial backing from an organization that lends venture capital – money that they are willing to risk in return for big rewards. The second strategy is to build on an existing successful business by adding an internet dimension. There is government and commercial help for such enterprises in the form of both advice and information. Government assistance is available at www.ukonlineforbusiness.gov.uk

see also...

Globalization; World Trade Organization

Economies and diseconomies of scale

When a business grows it has the chance to gain the benefits of *economies of scale*. Diseconomies are when the growth of the business causes problems. Some decisions to benefit from economies can be taken within the business. These are therefore called internal economies of scale. The main economies are financial, marketing, technical and risk-bearing.

- *Financial economies* are cost savings made such as being able to borrow both more money and more cheaply.
- *Marketing economies* include buying in bulk and spreading the costs of advertising.
- *Technical economies* include the use of specialist machines and workers, transport economies and the benefits of research and development.
- Bigger businesses can also spread risk over a larger output and over a greater variety of output, diversifying into other products.
- Diversification can also lead to diseconomies: if the business tries to do too many things at once it could end up doing none of them particularly well. Other diseconomies of scale are mainly managerial and organizational or linked to industrial relations.
- Managers may become less efficient and more remote from the business's operations, making them less effective.
- *Geographical diseconomies* occur where branches are so remote from each other and from head office that they do not feel part of the same organization.
- The management structure is likely to become more complex and therefore unwieldy. Lines of communication can become stretched and, as a consequence, decision making can become much less efficient.

External economies of scale are benefits that a business might gain from the growth of its industry. Many benefits are gained by having the industry concentrated in a particular geographical area, as a consequence, these economies may also be termed *economies of concentration.*

see also...

Business growth; Integration

Elasticity of demand

Elasticity of demand is the responsiveness of demand to a change in price. The concept has crossed from economics but is an important consideration for a business. Demand is the amount of a good or service which a consumer is willing to buy at a given price, in a given time period. The business needs to be able to estimate what will happen if it changes the price of a product. Sometimes a small change in price leads to a large change in demand. Sometimes a large change in price to only a small change in demand.

In the first case, the product may have many substitutes, so spending switches to these if price increases. Alternatively it may be a product where price has changed over a period of time, giving consumers the chance to make switches, or it may be a major part of a person's expenditure – a rise in the price of cars, for example, may mean that the purchase of a new car is put off. The proportionate fall in quantity demanded is greater than the proportionate fall in price – hence a drop in revenue. In the second case, the product either has no substitutes, or is a necessity, or makes up only a small percentage of a person's expenditure. Typical examples quoted are products such as salt and newspapers.

Such differences are of vital importance when a business is considering price changes. Take, for example, a single petrol station. If it raises the price of a litre of fuel, motorists will immediately switch to another station (petrol is a *homogeneous* good – in other words, one brand is a perfect substitute for another) and it will lose revenue. But the oil industry is another matter. They can raise prices (causing an increase at the pumps) because there is no substitute for their product. Many businesses go to great lengths to make their product as 'unique' and therefore as price inelastic as possible. Creating a brand image is just one example of this.

> ### see also...
> *Brand names and images; Demand*

Employment law

The Human Resources department in a business is responsible for issues connected with personnel such as health and safety and equality. It will be responsible for ensuring that the relevant Acts of Parliament are complied with.

The main law governing health and safety is the 1974 Health and Safety at Work Act. Many other rules and regulations are based on this legislation which is itself based on earlier legislation, in particular the 1961 Factories Act. This Act made provision for general health and safety issues such as proper washroom and toilet facilities, adequate ventilation, proper fire exits and comfortable levels of heating and lighting. It is also concerned with safety.

Employment law also covers equality. It states that in all matters of recruitment, selection, training, promotion opportunities, etc., there should be no discrimination on grounds of age, gender, race, religion, creed or sexual orientation. The main legislation is:

● 1970 Equal Pay Act. Men and women should receive equal pay for equal work.

● 1975 Sex Discrimination Act. This extended the law to take account of such things as recruitment and training and promotion opportunities.

● 1976 Race Relations Act. This made discrimination on the grounds of race or colour, marital status, nationality or ethnic group illegal and set up the Race Relations Board to investigate complaints.

● 1995 Disability Discrimination Act. Employers with 20 or more staff cannot discriminate against applicants or employees on grounds of disability, providing that they are capable of doing the job.

The government also ensures that legislation is passed to protect the rights of employees. This includes the right to join a trades union, the right to a statement of employment, the right to a certain amount of leave, to a pension, and to fair treatment. These were all brought up to date and into line with European legislation by the 1996 Employment Rights Act.

see also...

Recruitment; Employment law

Employment rights

Basic employment rights include the right to safe, healthy and reasonably comfortable working conditions. This includes the right to fair treatment.

The 1996 Employment Rights Act has been passed to ensure that Britain's employment laws are in line with those of the European Union and to ensure that workers receive fair treatment. The Act outlines a number of rights:

1 All employees are entitled to a statement of their employment details which must be written and must contain details such as rates of pay, terms and conditions of employment, pensions, notice periods, disciplinary procedures and so on. If a statement is not issued within two months of the employment starting, then the employee can take the employer to an industrial tribunal who will rule on what the conditions should be – a ruling that is binding on the employer.

2 All employees have the right to an itemized pay statement.

3 All employees and employers have the right to a minimum notice period on either side.

4 If dismissed, all employees are entitled to a written statement of the reasons for their dismissal.

5 Employees have the right not to be unfairly dismissed. This particularly includes paragraphs covering the return to work after childbirth.

6 Employees can appeal to an industrial tribunal if they feel they have been unfairly dismissed and the tribunal can, if it finds in their favour, order the employer to reinstate the employee in a position and at a level as if they had never been dismissed.

7 Employees have the right to redundancy payments.

Many of these provisions could pose particular problems for a small employer such as a sole trader. Perhaps because of this, many sole traders either do not employ anyone or employ only a minimum number of people, relying on short-term contracts or freelancers to fill gaps when necessary.

see also...

Recruitment; Employment law

Enterprise

Enterprise is all about risk taking. An entrepreneur does not know for sure whether a product will sell and will have risked time and probably money in order to get it to a stage where it is ready for sale. The entrepreneur is therefore often referred to as a risk taker; the reward for taking such risk is profit.

The UK is said to have developed an enterprise economy in the early twenty-first century. This means that entrepreneurs are encouraged by government and other institutions to start businesses and that the contribution of the small business to the economy is recognized. Encouraging enterprise results in many more people being self-employed, in the creation of jobs and in a vibrant and forward-looking economy. Other benefits include new products and processes being developed and launched and unemployment being reduced. People who work for themselves in an enterprise economy are likely to have much greater motivation than those who work for others as they will benefit more directly from the success of their own business than from the success of an employer's.

Government sees the benefits of encouraging enterprise as lower unemployment and less reliance on state benefits but also as providing better products and a better standard of service to consumers.

Government and other institutions provide help and advice for entrepreneurs. For example, the Loan Guarantee Scheme is operated by the government.

There are also private organizations which encourage enterprise. The Prince's Youth Business Trust provides advice and help (including financial help) to young people wishing to set up in business, while The Small Business Bureau is particularly concerned with helping young women in business through its 'Women into Business' scheme.

Enterprise involves risk and therefore also involves failure – over 50 per cent of small businesses fail within two years of starting.

see also...

Personalities; Small business

European Union

The European Union grew out of the post-war belief that, if the countries of Europe were trading together, there would be less likelihood of further wars. The EU has grown in stages to its current 2001 membership of 15 nations, with many others (particularly from Eastern Europe) applying to join. The purpose of the Union is to establish a free trade area in Europe, with no internal barriers to trade and common standards (harmonization). Most members also believed that monetary union was desirable (some even advocate ultimate political union). In 1986 its members accepted that an acceleration to full harmonization was needed and set 1992 as the date for achieving this. The Single European Market, with most harmonization complete and border controls removed, was established on January 1 1993. For business this meant the harmonization of many safety and technical standards, making it easier for businesses to operate. For individuals, regulations cover consumer protection, and the rights of employees. Goods coming into the Union are subject to a tariff. This, firstly, increases the price of imported goods, encouraging demand to stay within the EU, secondly it encourages businesses to source from within the Union wherever possible.

The Maastricht Treaty of 1991 was designed to increase the pace of harmonization. It included the Social Chapter which, as well as confirming social rights for workers contains provisions to promote more worker involvement in businesses through, for example, worker councils.

The European Union affects business in a number of major ways. It provides businesses within the Union with a larger market (the Single Market) of some 360 million people. The movement of labour and capital within the Union has also become much easier. This means that businesses can locate where labour is cheaper or labour can move to where there are employment opportunities. Other advantages include a greater range of sources of finance for business.

see also...

EU institutions; EU policies and European Monetary Union

European Union institutions

The European Union is governed by its three main institutions: the European Commission, the European Council of Ministers and the European Parliament.

The *European Commission* is the policy-making body of the Union. It takes an overview of developments and problems and proposes policies and solutions. Its members are not elected but appointed by member states. France, Germany, Italy, Spain and the UK are allocated two Commissioners each due to the size of their populations; the other members get one. 1999 saw a great deal of controversy attaching itself to the Commissioners, who were forced to resign due to irregularities with the budget. One of the problems of the EU has been the lack of accountability of members of the European Commission.

The *European Council of Ministers* is constituted when ministers from member countries meet to formulate policy. There is no permanent membership of this body, membership is made up of the ministers of EU countries. Often meetings of this body are referred to as 'summit' meetings. When the prime ministers of member states meet the body effectively becomes the cabinet of the EU. The EU presidency is the chair of this group with the office rotating around the countries of the EU on a half-yearly basis so that each member takes a turn at providing the president of the European Council.

The *European Parliament* has 626 directly elected members, with numbers again allocated according to the size of population of member states (the UK has 87 members). Members are elected by proportional representation at a European ballot held every five years. This is the legislative or law-making body of the EU which is gradually becoming a more powerful body.

The European Court of Justice decides on disputes which arise involving national laws and EU laws.

see also...

Eurpean Union; EU policies and European Monetary Union

European Union policies

One of the main planks of EU policy has been the Common Agricultural Policy. This policy was introduced to help farmers by guaranteeing prices. If an excess of agricultural goods is produced, the European Union buys up the excess in order to prevent prices to farmers falling. This bulk purchase is triggered when the price falls to a particular level called the *intervention price*. Historically, the intervention price has been set at too high a level which has led to large stocks of various agricultural goods – wine, butter and grain amongst them – being built up and having to be sold off cheaply outside the Union – against a lot of opposition to the from consumers within the Union.

European Regional Policy helps those regions where traditional industry has declined and where unemployment is high: while the European Social Fund is used primarily to pay for retraining and regeneration programmes. Regional funding is also available to help develop transport and infrastructure.

The Social Chapter is the part of the Maastricht Treaty that is designed to harmonize worker conditions throughout the Union. The main new rights for UK workers involved the minimum wage and worker participation in decision making.

European Monetary Union is the idea that, ultimately, the countries of the European Union will use the same currency. This will remove the costs of currency transactions, increase the flow of trade and ensure that economies are growing at the same rate. The European Central Bank has been established as the central bank of the Union, but worries about this include either that it will be too powerful and override national interests in the interest of the 'European' economy, or (from other quarters) that it will not be powerful enough.

---

see also...

European Union; EU institutions and European Monetary Union

European Monetary Union

A single currency is one of the aims of the European Union. This currency, to be called the Euro, will replace domestic currencies in the member countries. The UK is still outside the single currency area, preferring to wait until economic conditions are right before joining.

There are arguments for and against the single currency. The two opposing camps are usually referred to as Europhiles and Eurosceptics. *Europhiles* are for full integration of the UK into the Union, including monetary union, believing that Britain can be a stronger force for control and reform of the Union if it is inside it. *Eurosceptics*, on the other hand, believe that a cautious and gradual approach to the Union is better. Many Eurosceptics are sceptical enough to want to avoid monetary union and keep sterling.

The Labour government has been pragmatic about European Monetary Union, laying down five economic conditions to be met before Britain should consider membership. These conditions are: whether business cycles and economic structures are compatible, whether the system is sufficiently flexible to deal with problems, the impact on long-term investment and whether joining would promote growth and employment. Should the conditions be met, then the final decision would still rest with the electorate, who would be asked about monetary union in a referendum.

The single currency has a major benefit to business (and overseas travellers) in that currency charges and associated commissions are not incurred. It should also make trade easier and smoother as prices, quoted in a common currency, should be better understood by all trading parties. The second major benefit is in the stability of the currency. Because the combined economies of the European Union states are so strong, there should be little room for currency fluctuations.

see also...

European Union; EU institutions and EU policies

Factors of production

The factors of production are those inputs that are required to produce a business output, either a good or a service. There are three factors which are *land*, *labour*, and *capital*, that are paid for and organized by the 'fourth factor' of enterprise. The fourth factor may be considered as the most important of the factors of production as, without the *risk taking and organizational skills* of the entrepreneur, the other factors would be useless. It is the entrepreneur who decides on the nature of the business enterprise, the amounts and types of factors that will be necessary and then obtains the finance to buy the factors.

For some businesses' land – which includes buildings – is going to be more costly than for others, but no business can operate without a base of some sort. The return to land is rent. What this means is that the income that a business would earn from the ownership of land, or the cost of using land, is termed as rent.

The second factor is *labour*. This means any sort of human effort, whether by hand or brain, that is used in the production of a good or service, not just physical labour. The return to labour is wages and salaries.

Capital is the plant, equipment, machinery and tools used to produce a good or service. It is not, as is often wrongly quoted, money. The 'capital' of a business actually refers to the saleable assets of that business. The return to capital is interest.

It is the mixture of land, labour and capital required that is important to a business. Some businesses will be 'capital intensive', i.e. require a lot of machinery, plant, etc.; others will be 'labour intensive', relying heavily on human effort. This may have implications for where a business may locate globally. For example, a labour-intensive industry may locate in a poorer country with lower labour charges and less labour organization and regulation.

see also...
Enterprise; Productive efficiency

Financial accounting

Financial accounting looks at the past flows of money into and out of the business – it is concerned with what has already happened and therefore serves to give a historical picture of a business. Companies must produce financial accounts and make them available to the public according to the terms of the Companies Act. In the case of *private limited companies*, these are likely to be basic accounts, giving the minimum of information; in the case of a *public limited company*, they are likely to be a great deal more detailed. Indeed, one of the reasons why so many sole traders and partnerships do not become companies and take advantage of limited liability is because of the requirement for transparency in financial dealings.

Financial accounts are governed by financial and accounting conventions which detail the way in which the accounts should be presented.

Accounting conventions are designed to ensure that managers can measure one set of accounts against another knowing that figures have been entered according to the same criteria: consistency, matching, materiality, prudence and realization. *Consistency* means that whatever methodology is adopted, this should always be used so that the accounts from one accounting period can be directly compared with those from another. *Matching* means that revenues and expenses are allocated when a benefit or cost is felt by the organization. *Materiality* means that only important costs and revenues material to the accounts are included (e.g. expenditure on tea for workers would not be included). *Prudence* means that accounts should be compiled as cautiously as possible. Finally, *realization* is that profit is realized when a sale or delivery is made, not when it is actually paid for.

The three main financial accounting documents are the *cash flow statement*; the *profit and loss account* and the *balance sheet*.

see also...

Cash flow forecast; Profit and loss account; Balance sheet

Floating a company

Flotation is part of the process of becoming a public limited company. It is a way of raising money from people who have confidence in the future of the company and are willing to back this with money.

Achieving company status, or *incorporation*, means that the company is a separate legal entity from its owners, it can act and be acted on in law in its own name and it can be bought and sold. Shareholders in a company benefit from limited liability.

A company is formed by the process of incorporation. Its owners send a Memorandum of Association and Articles of Association to the Registrar of Companies at Companies House in Cardiff. The memorandum shows the name and location of the company and its objectives, the names of directors and the amount of capital it has, divided into how many shares. The articles are the internal rules of the company such as how directors may be elected or meetings called.

To float a company involves the preparation of a prospectus. This is like a brochure which is issued to attract investors to buy shares in the company. It will contain a summary of the activities of the company, a history and a summation of the company's accounts. Shares are offered for sale to the public via the prospectus.

The main advantage of floating a company is in the amount of money that can be raised on the Stock Exchange. A publicly quoted company must have a minimum of £50,000 share capital. Publicly quoted companies also tend to get more publicity than those that aren't. The downside includes having to reveal many more financial and accounting details than non-public companies, and the possibility of losing control of the business. Once shares are issued, they can be sold on to anyone, so could be bought by a competitor or rival who, once they have bought a certain number of shares, can bid for the remainder of the shares and take over the company.

see also...

Shares; Stakeholders; Privatisation; Liability

Forecasting

Businesses need to estimate what might happen in a future situation. To do this they use current financial figures and statistical tools in order to forecast the future, to help with their planning.

Cash flow forecasts are part of management accounting and are used to give the business an idea of how much money it is likely to need and when it is likely to need it. Sales forecasts are used so that the business can plan how much it needs to produce (and therefore what materials to buy) plus stock and staffing levels. Profit and loss forecasts are important for a business to be able to decide on future policy.

Forecasting techniques in business are usually one of three kinds – extrapolation from trends, probability or Delphi technique.

Extrapolating from trends means following the likely path of a factor. This can predict the future accurately in some situations, but this is not always the case. The figure shows the general changes in UK interest rates from 1989 to 2001. A forecaster could have looked at the trend in 1997 and been forgiven for concluding that (as the dotted line shows) interest rates would continue to rise into 1999 and 2000. However, due to a combination of other factors (the main one being the 1997 general election) interest rates actually fell.

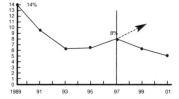

Probability involves predicting future events on the basis of events that have taken place – a bit like backing a racehorse on its previous form. The *Delphi technique* is named after the famous oracle at Delphi, where a priestess of Apollo predicted the future. It uses panels of experts to forecast changes.

see also...

Statistics; Variances

43

Franchises

Franchises are a way of starting, owning and operating a business without the high levels of risk associated with other start-ups. Less than one in 15 franchise outlets actually stops trading in any one year and nine out of ten are profitable. Compared with the failure rate of most small businesses – over half cease trading in their first two years – this is phenomenally successful.

When buying a franchise you buy into the success of an established business. You buy the use of its name, its brand, its advertising, its reputation and its support. It is not a form of business ownership, but of operation.

The franchiser (a word often spelt in its archaic form of franchisor) is the seller of the franchise. It is the business that has a successful product, brand or format. It sells franchises to franchisees. A franchise is permission to sell the product or brand, to use the format, or, in some cases, to provide the particular service. Well-known high street franchise operations include Pizza Hut, The Body Shop, BSM (British School of Motoring) and McDonald's.

Franchisers charge a fee for the franchise and collect a royalty, usually based on the annual sales of the franchisee. In return for the fees and royalties the franchisee buys into an established business and may receive help with products, staff, training, marketing and sales materials. Franchisers may be quite restrictive – insisting on particular suppliers, making sure that uniforms, products and services are identical and curtailing any attempt to expand or augment a range.

Franchises are also sold by the government or agencies for certain services. Train operators have to buy the franchise to provide particular services; television and radio broadcasters buy the franchise to provide the service in a particular area or over a particular wavelength. Effectively, these franchises say that 'xyz business has the right to broadcast programmes/provide train services in this region/under these circumstances'.

see also...
Private business ownership

44

Globalization

This is the process by which a company decides to focus on global markets rather than on domestic ones.

Global distribution is usually achieved by promoting a global brand. This means ensuring that the same product, service, etc., is available in the same format throughout the globe. In other cases, the brand may provide an 'umbrella' for a variety of different products, such as Sony.

Many companies which operate on a global basis are multi-nationals or trans-national companies, with plant and operations in many countries. This allows them to move investments to keep both costs and taxation low and often puts them outside national laws. They will also have powers of leverage over governments in being able to promise investment and jobs in certain areas (usually for certain concessions). Historically, many countries protected their home trade against competition but agreements on reducing protection through GATT and the World Trade Organization have led to freer trade.

Global location may be to take advantage of lower labour costs, or less organized labour or of lower taxation. This has brought trans-nationals and the whole concept of globalization into conflict with human rights groups, who see global concerns exploiting labour or natural resources in poorer countries in order to boost profits in richer ones. Global concerns can also sometimes decide where to pay their taxes to take advantage of different rates.

The major criticisms of global organizations centre on the way they exploit resources in certain countries and use undue influence in other countries. Companies have been accused of destroying the environment and exploiting labour for profit, as well as supporting certain governments and opposing others for their own advantage. The real criticism is that global concerns are accountable to no one but their own shareholders.

see also...

Branding; World Trade Organization

Government policies

There are many specific government policies which affect business, such as on levels of business taxation, or on grants or other start-up schemes that are available. There is also a whole raft of laws to regulate and control business for the benefit of employers, employees and consumers. Governments directly influence business through their own expenditure on goods and services: government is a major direct purchaser of roads, public buildings and defence and indirectly affects levels of demand through providing pensions and other state benefits. It both spends itself and encourages expenditure through regional policy, and channels EU regional funds.

The generally accepted aims of government are full employment, economic growth, no or low inflation and a favourable balance of payments. Governments can influence each of these through fiscal and monetary policy.

Fiscal policy is carried out through changes in direct government spending and taxation. This means that fiscal policy can be reasonably accurately targeted. The size of the Public Sector Borrowing Requirement (PSBR) can also be used as a tool for policy. This is the amount of money that governments have to borrow to make up the shortfall between expenditure and revenue. If the government needs to borrow money – i.e. attract money from investors – then this puts upward pressure on interest rates. Higher interest rates have a detrimental effect on business.

Monetary policy involves the control of the money supply. This, effectively, means the amount of borrowing in the economy and the main policy tool was interest rates. These are now (since 1997) changed by the Bank of England for economic reasons, not by the government. There are other monetary policy tools (such as buying and selling sterling on the open market) that are available to governments.

see also...

ACAS; Industrial relations; Consumer protection; Trade cycle

Human resource management

Human resource management (HRM) has grown from the old personnel function to mean the way in which staff can be used as a strategic resource to enhance the efficiency, profitability and performance of a business. HRM thus includes involvement at all levels of an employee's recruitment, selection and retention. The path through a business should be as shown in the figure.

Recruitment and selection involves prior workforce planning, so that the HR manager knows the type and calibre of staff that is needed. This involves a process of job analysis in order to create a person specification. This is the detailed description of the ideal candidate for the post, listing the essential and desirable characteristics required. The selection process then involves advertising the post, short-listing candidates so that a manageable number are invited to interview, and then interviewing.

Training and development will take different forms depending on the appointee's stage in his/her career. All new appointments to a business will require some form of induction training. This is training to introduce staff to the workplace, the job and to custom and practice in the business. Further training may be on or off the job, i.e. at the place of work, whilst working, or at an external institution. At a later date an employee will go through an appraisal process. This should be used as a strategic tool to make sure that the employee is performing to levels that will help the business to reach its objectives.

The final stage of HRM is retirement. In a company which practices HRM policies, benefits for retired workers are good and they are still treated as part of the business, part of 'the family'. This is part of the reward for loyal service to the business.

see also...

Appraisal; Lean production; Motivation theories

Industrial relations

Industrial relations refers to the relationship and to the various negotiations and agreements between employers and employees. Employees are usually (but not always) represented by a trades union or professional association; employers may represent themselves or be represented by an employers' association. The negotiations and discussions are usually on wages or conditions and, because they are taking place between representatives of groups, are called *collective bargaining*.

A breakdown of industrial relations means that a form of disagreement has broken out between an employer and a group of employees and that an industrial dispute is therefore in progress. An industrial dispute will often mean that some kind of industrial action is taken by one side or the other. Types of industrial action range in seriousness from minor irritations to all-out strikes. The main types of action from the employees' side are overtime bans, working to rule (production will be slowed if all rules and regulations are followed to the letter) and go-slows (continuing with the job but at a much reduced rate). As an ultimate weapon, employees can withdraw their labour altogether in a strike. Strikes may be selective, short (one-day strikes) or total and will be damaging to both employers and employees. On the employers' side, those in dispute may, in certain cases, be dismissed or the employer may refuse to allow them to work (a 'lock out'). Because such tactics are so damaging, there are mechanisms in place to try to stop industrial disputes escalating.

Legislation provides a framework within which industrial relations are conducted, establishing the rights of employers and employees.

Should a breakdown be inevitable, there are bodies in place to help. Industrial tribunals may be used to give a ruling when a dispute arises that is covered by law. The main body is the Advisory, Conciliation and Arbitration Service (ACAS), which provides a service to help solve industrial disputes through negotiation and agreement.

see also...

ACAS; Government policies

Industrial sectors

Industry is divided into sectors relating to the operating stages of the production process. A product normally goes through a production process which involves raw materials, processing or manufacturing, distribution and retailing. This means that the raw materials have to be extracted or otherwise obtained; factories and plant are needed for manufacturing; various commercial functions (such as transport and insurance) are necessary before the good reaches the final consumer.

The first stage of the process is called *primary production*. This involves the extraction of raw materials. It therefore includes fishing, farming and forestry along with the more obvious mining, quarrying and drilling.

Secondary industry involves taking the raw materials and turning them into finished or part-finished goods. It therefore involves processes such as refining, processing and manufacture.

Tertiary industry is not just the final stage in a product's life – from manufacturer to wholesaler, retailer and consumer – but also refers to all of the other services which are provided to support primary and secondary industry. Insurance, banking, communications and other support services are all part of the tertiary sector (along with direct services such as transport and retailing).

The stage of development that a country has reached is sometimes measured in terms of its reliance on various industries. The figure shows the difference in emphasis between the different sectors as a country develops. The UK is an example of the third type of country.

PRIMARY
raw materials
↓
SECONDARY
manufacturing/processing
↓
TERTIARY
services

see also...

Factors of production

49

Integration

This is one of the ways in which a business may grow. It means one business joining with another by either merger or take-over.

Mergers are where the two companies are equal partners and agree to join together. *Take-overs* are where one company buys out another. This may be an agreed bid or it may be a hostile take-over, involving the company buying shares in its target acquisition.

The various types of integration are categorized according to where each business is in the chain of production. *Vertical integration* means joining with a company in a similar business but at a different place in the chain. An example would be a brewery buying a hop supplier or a brewery buying a public house. The first is backward vertical integration, the second is forward vertical integration. *Horizontal integration* involves two businesses at the same level of production – one brewer merging with another, for example. *Lateral integration* is merging with a firm whose products may be bought as complementary products. An

example could be a brewery joining with a crisp or peanut manufacturer, a soft drinks manufacturer, or a distillery. *Conglomerate integration* is where there is no connection between the two businesses. It is also called *diversification* as it means that the businesses are entering completely different markets. An example might be of a brewery buying a book publishers.

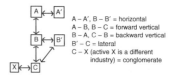

A – A', B – B' = horizontal
A – B, B – C = forward vertical
B – A, C – B = backward vertical
B' – C = lateral
C – X (active X is a different industry) = conglomerate

see also...

Business growth; Economies and diseconomies of scale

International trade

International trade refers to the trade between different nations. There are a number of reasons for international trade. Firstly, that certain products can be produced economically only in certain countries, either because they are found there (diamonds in South Africa, opals in Australia) or because local conditions are necessary for production (rubber, for example). Secondly, there is the case that, even though more than one country can produce a good, one has a comparative advantage over the other. This may be because of labour conditions or the environment which favours production (cotton and bananas are two products of which this is true).

The country which has the comparative advantage in the production of a product should specialize in it and trade with other countries for other products. In this way there will be more goods and services available to consumers, and at cheaper prices. Other advantages of international trade to businesses are that they can sell their products in a much wider market.

Trade may be free trade, i.e. subject to no restrictions, or trade that is policed or restricted in some way. The main restrictions on trade are *quotas*, a limit on the amount of goods which may be imported and *tariffs*, an extra tax placed on imported goods to make them less attractive to consumers than domestic products. Other barriers include technical ones, such as insisting that cars be engineered to a particular standard or straightforward embargoes – an *embargo* means that importing a particular product is forbidden. For example, there is an embargo in the UK on trade in ivory and other products of rare species. Governments can intervene through the use of *exchange controls* – limiting the amount of currency that can be bought and sold therefore limiting trade – and through *subsidies* – giving grants or other support to domestic industries to help them against foreign competition.

---

see also...

Balance of Payments; European Union

Investment appraisal

nvestment appraisal is the process by which a business decides whether a large-scale project can be afforded. Businesses will look at the projected cost of the project, at the possible risk factors, and at the benefits that might accrue. The process means that one project can be compared against another and a judgement made as to which is likely to be the most successful.

For any sort of capital project, a business needs to make capital investment decisions. This means that they have to estimate future costs from the base of current costs and try to accurately forecast the levels of future revenues. Costs can only be estimated using current prices; revenues must be estimated over the projected life span. Businesses use four main techniques to make such estimates as accurate as possible. These are Average Rate of Return (ARR), Payback, Net Present Value (NPV) and Internal Rate of Return (IRR).

ARR looks at the likely returns the business will get from a completed project over its forecast life span. If the returns will be greater than the cost, in a short enough time period,

the project can go ahead. *Payback* estimates the length of time it will take for the business to recover its cost in revenues. *NPV* links the value of returns to predicted inflation rates. It also takes into account predictions on currency fluctuations. Future returns are estimated and then reduced in accordance with predictions regarding the spending power of money in the future. This is called discounting the cash flow. Businesses will also compare possible discounted rates of return with predictions of what could be gained from safe investments. *IRR* approaches the problem in the same way as NPV, but from the other direction. It looks for the point in the project life span at which NPV is zero and then calculates the interest rate that would be necessary to get the same return.

The major drawback of investment appraisal is that it is based on predictions and forecasts.

see also...

Cost benefit analysis; Location of business

Japanese methodologies

In the 1970s many western businesses felt that they were losing out to Japanese competition as Japan outstripped them in terms of innovation, production and productivity. Much of the advantage was put down to the introduction of Japanese production techniques. These techniques crossed to the West, the most notable ones being Kaizen, just-in-time (or lean production) and quality circles.

Toyota, after the Second World War, studied American mass production methods at Ford and found them to be highly inefficient. They recognized faults and set up a system which removed as many of them as possible – in particular concentrating on training labour better and to having production lines that could react quickly to changes in demand (flexible production). The Americans, worried by Japan's seeming dominance by the 1980s, set up a study to learn from the Japanese and coined the term 'lean production' for these methods. Lean production (qv) was in addition to the central Japanese concept of gradual improvement (Kaizen) through the involvement of the workers.

Kaizen means 'continuous improvement' and involves evolution rather than revolution. It can be seen as a refinement of value analysis in that every part of a production process, and the use of all the inputs, is continuously being looked at to see if even the slightest improvement can be made. Western companies have tended to expand or re-tool in 'leaps', using new or improved technology. This process was termed Business Process Engineering (BPE) in the 1990s.

Kaizen is a process of gradual improvement. It involves the workforce in generating ideas for small improvements which can easily be implemented. The system has, as its biggest advantage, the fact that gradual change is not disruptive.

see also...

Lean production

Leadership styles

Managers in organizations operate particular leadership styles – if they are good managers they will vary the style according to the situation. The main styles identified are autocratic, *laissez-faire*, democratic, bureaucratic and paternalistic. There are also sub-divisions and variations of each style.

Autocratic leaders instruct and direct and do not require subordinate input. *Laissez-faire* managers are the opposite of this, allowing subordinates to express views and argue a case. This can be more motivating but lead to a lack of central direction or purpose – managers may even be pulling in different directions. The *democratic* leadership style, where subordinates are allowed to participate in decision making, should lead to more motivation and job satisfaction, but may also prove long-winded and inefficient.

Bureaucratic decision making is where decisions are made according to a rigid set of rules – this stifles both interest and innovation. It means that, rather than take responsibility themselves, managers delegate the decision making to the rule book. This tends to lead to organizations that are inflexible and lack dynamism. The *paternalistic* style is where managers take (or think that they are taking) the welfare of workers into account when making decisions. The main drawback of this approach is that what 'father' thinks is good for the workers, may not be what they think is good!

Tannenbaum and Schmidt propose a range of management styles, (as shown in the figure), which correspond with some of these main styles.

Democratic / Autocratic chart showing: 1 tell, 1 sell, 1 trust, 1 consult, 1 share

see also...

Management theorists

Lean production

Lean production is the overall concept of improving productive efficiency by minimizing the use of all the inputs necessary for production – cutting down on the use of raw materials, labour, land (in terms of factory space and efficiency of use), capital and, perhaps most importantly, the time taken for an operation. It is a system which attempts to keep stock levels at a minimum and lead-in and development times as short as possible. The main version of lean production is the just-in-time (JIT) approach which contrasts with the traditional 'just in case' approach.

JIT production involves stock arriving just in time to be used in the production process. This has advantages in terms of not holding stock but disadvantages if suppliers are unreliable.

Stocks are only ordered in anticipation of them being needed by the production process. No stock is kept in storage 'just in case'. Stocks are therefore not 'pushed' through the production line, i.e. ordered, stored and then used as needed. Instead they are said to be 'pulled through' the system – they are only ordered just before they are needed by managers on the spot. The system is reliant on short and reliable 'lead-in' times – the time it takes for stock to be delivered. One example of the system is the 'two bin' approach (called Kanban). As the supply of materials (in bin 1) falls to a certain level, this triggers the order of more stock (bin 2). Bin 2 is timed to arrive exactly as bin 1 is emptied so that there is only ever one bin in use.

All parts of a business should use lean production techniques where possible. This includes the development of new product lines. Simultaneous engineering means that representatives from all parts of the production process meet together to develop new products. This includes marketing and production as well as the design and development team. In this way, problems that might have occurred at a later stage can be ironed out early because the expertise is there to spot them.

see also...

Japanese methodologies; TQM

55

Liability

Liability is the responsibility of the owner of a business for the debts of that business. Owners may be totally responsible or may be able to limit their liability, hence the major division in types of business organization between limited liability companies and those owners with unlimited liability.

The owners of businesses trading as sole traders and partnerships are fully and completely liable for the debts of their respective enterprises 'up to the limit of their financial wealth'. Should the business run up debts which it is unable to repay, the creditors of the business (those to whom the business owes money) can take the business to court and have the owner made bankrupt. If the court agrees to issue a bankruptcy order then the business owner can be obliged to sell personal possessions in order to pay the debt. Possessions and business assets may even be seized by bailiffs appointed by the court and sold at auction in order to raise money. Only when the bankrupt can show that all debts have been repaid will the court discharge them. As a sole trader it is the single owner who carries this liability. In a partnership the partners are jointly and severally liable unless they have limited liability by opting to be a silent partner – putting money into the business but taking no part in its running.

By becoming a limited company, the business person can limit their liability for the debts of the business to the amount of money that they originally put into it. All limited companies carry a warning in their name that they have limited liability, so that anyone dealing with the company will know that they are taking a risk. In a private limited company this is contained in the 'Limited' (usually shortened to Ltd.) that must follow the name of the company; in a public limited company it is in the PLC abbreviation which, again, must always follow the name of the company.

> ### see also...
> *Small business; Floating a company*

Location of business

For a business supplying directly to consumers, location factors are going to include accessibility, local services, rates and rents and the presence of competition. Businesses locate in areas where there is competition rather than away from it, as they have a better chance of drawing customers if they do so. Certain services will be located as near to customers as possible, for example, the service provided by a local shop, bank or hairdressers. In other cases, the service will be located at a particular place due to geographical factors (holiday destinations) or due to the specialist nature of the service (you would not expect a heart surgeon to come to you). Such products are said to be *market oriented*.

Deciding where to produce or manufacture a product is influenced by other factors. In particular how near production needs to be to raw materials, or how near to consumers. There will be a certain amount of 'pull' in both directions. A bulk decreasing industry will need to do its processing or manufacture as near to its source of raw materials and components as possible. Bulk decreasing means that the good gets either smaller in size or more compact or becomes easier to transport once it is processed. Oil refining is an example. A bulk increasing industry will need to be located near its market.

Other factors to take into account include the cost, size and suitability of land, labour and government or other external assistance. The availability of natural resources may also be an important factor (coconuts don't grow in Iceland) plus the quality of the site and availability of infrastructure (power, transport links, etc.) The size, quality and structure of the labour force needed, which will also affect its cost, is also important. Government help may come in the form of grants, subsidies, lower taxes or rates or advice and other external bodies (such as the European Union) may also provide benefits to encourage businesses to locate in certain areas.

---

see also...

Cost benefit analysis; Investment appraisal

Management accounting

Management accounting involves the internal financial information available to managers, as opposed to that information which must be published by law. This is information kept as part of the finance function and is used for forward planning, reviewing and analysis of the performance of the business. Essentially, financial accounting is concerned with the past revenues and expenditures of the business, while management accounting is concerned with the future. As such it is one of the most important tools used in strategic planning.

Management accounting involves the classification of costs and revenues and the setting of budgets. The flows of revenue and expenditure are shown on a cash flow forecast. This is used to predict future flows of cash into a business so that plans can be made for borrowing when necessary or for investing money if there is going to be a cash surplus. Where financial accounting is concerned with a cash flow statement (a snapshot), management accounting makes a forecast.

Managers can also use figures on projected sales and revenues to produce a break-even chart to calculate the number of sales needed for revenue to match costs. This will be closely linked to the setting of budgets which can be broken down by plant, process or department. Budgets are an important part of the management function, as a way to control and co-ordinate levels of expenditure in an organization. Break even can also be calculated through the *contribution method*. Contribution statements can be linked to cost and profit centres for more efficient management.

The final tool of management accounting is investment appraisal, a technique used to evaluate the likely costs and returns of large-scale capital projects.

see also...

Break even; Cash flow forecast; Investment appraisal

Management theorists

Business theory began to develop seriously in the twentieth century as first mass production and then the pressures of competition began to force managers to think about better and more efficient ways of achieving objectives. Many of the contributions outlined below are covered in greater detail in fuller entries under either the theory or the theorist's name. Motivational theorists are listed separately under motivation.

Igor Ansoff (1918–) contributed to the study of strategic planning. In particular he introduced, in 1965, the Ansoff matrix which attempts to measure the possible risks and rewards of launching new products. He has been criticized for advocating a set approach to strategy rather than taking account of changing circumstances.

W. Edward Deming (1900–1993) is known as the father of total quality management (TQM) – the idea that everyone is responsible for quality at every stage of production.

Peter Drucker (1909–) introduced the idea of management by objectives (MBO). This involves managers setting clear targets or steps to an ultimate objective. He developed many of his ideas by conducting case studies of large corporations such as General Motors and IBM.

Charles Handy (1932–). Professor Handy developed theories on organizational cultures whilst an executive with BP.

Henry Minzberg (1939–) is a Canadian academic who studied what managers actually do rather than what theorists said they were supposed to do. He believes that the dynamics of business are more important than defining an organizational structure; the opposite to Ansoff.

Tom Peters (1942–) is probably the widest read of the current business gurus. Peters analyzed 43 top companies that had been successful over a period of time to identify the factors which led to their success.

> ## see also...
>
> *Ansoff matrix; Peters, Tom; Shamrock theory; Total Quality Management*

Managers and management functions

Managers are so important to business that they have occupied the minds of theorists and writers probably more than any other area of business.

Henri Fayol described the higher order functions of management as being able to plan, organize, delegate, command, co-ordinate and control.

Some modern methods of management do away with the manager and, instead, put teams in charge of their own decision making. Once objectives have been agreed (and here senior management may still need to be involved) the other management functions devolve to the team, who are empowered to make the necessary decisions to reach the target. This has the advantage of being motivating and of using the expertise within the team: its disadvantage lies in the possibility of having many teams all seeking to reach different targets. A management overview (and the control and co-ordination that goes with such an overview) may still be necessary.

Variations of this approach include quality circles and MBO. Quality circles (this is part of total quality management) are groups of workers who meet, in company time, to provide a consultative background of opinion and innovation to management. MBO – Management by Objectives – involves managers communicating objectives to workers for them to agree so that they and management have joint ownership of the objectives.

Contingency theory suggests that different management styles should be adopted to suit particular circumstances. Variables may include the time scale, the actual task to be completed, the materials and equipment available, the amount and quality of labour and the corporate culture of the organization.

see also...

Decision making; Management theorists; Leadership styles

Managing change

Changes to a business organization can improve its competitive position and performance or debilitate or destroy the organization. Which of these two actually happens depends on the organization's ability to manage change. Change may be internal or external, unforeseen or predictable. *Internal* changes are within the control of the business, *external* outside of its control. Some changes are expected and forecast (a trend in demand toward or away from certain products, for example) while some may be totally unpredictable (such as the emergence and success of a new product or innovation).

Organizations can manage change by ensuring that they are the driving force behind the change. This is called a *proactive approach* and means that the organization is in charge of its own destiny. However, in opting to change in a certain direction, the business may fall foul of external factors that it was unable to predict. It is therefore important that the business is flexible, able to alter course to take new factors and circumstances into account.

Managing unplanned change would mean that the business has a *reactive approach*. This means that they wait for change to happen and then try to alter course to meet the challenge of the change. This approach is a more cautious one than the proactive one, as businesses should know which factors are likely to affect them before initiating change. However, it can also lead to a pattern of decline and recovery that is uncertain and hampers the efficiency of the organization.

Management skills in introducing change include being able to empathize with others' concerns and introducing change in a sensitive way. However, if change is inevitable, hard decisions (such as redundancies) should be made quickly and with clear reasons, rather than being drawn out. The ability to manage change can be vital to a business's success.

see also...

Communication; Leadership styles

Market failure

In a market price is set by the operation of demand and supply – if there is a shortage and high demand, price will rise; a surplus and it will fall. Markets should balance supply and demand so that they 'clear', i.e. all the products are bought at an agreed price. When markets fail to clear we say that there has been market failure.

Market failure may happen for a number of reasons, amongst them: it may not be possible to set an economic price for the product, people's needs may be considered more important than price, or businesses may gain control of a market. If there is market failure, it is often the role of governments to intervene. For example, local councils may provide goods for which an economic price cannot be charged such as street lighting, or social products such as education; farm prices may be subsidized to guarantee farmers' incomes.

It may be in the interests of businesses to engineer market failure. A group of businesses dominating a market is called an oligopoly (such as the Seven Sisters, the world's major oil companies). They can decide to operate as a cartel by fixing prices so that there is no competition. A single business with sufficient power to fix prices or supply in its market is termed a monopoly. Governments may intervene to prevent or control businesses who have taken control of a market through the Competition Commission and the Office of Fair Trading or prohibit mergers or take-overs taking place that might cause such a market failure.

Sometimes market failure comes about as a result of government intervention – where there is no price mechanism (the operation of supply and demand) present, then other ways of allocation will develop. The National Health Service operates on the basis of queuing, allocation might also take place through rationing.

Interventions are not always successful and many businesses believe that competition – and allowing markets to clear at whatever price – is the most efficient way of operation.

see also...

Competition Commission

Market planning

Market planning is how a business decides on its marketing objectives and the best way in which it might achieve them. Various techniques have been developed to help businesses with such planning, which are based on various analyses and interpretations of prevailing market conditions.

Each business will be looking to target a particular consumer or group of consumers, so part of marketing planning may be to build up a consumer profile of the target group. The profile will be linked to the consumer's potential spending power. Businesses may build up a profile of an ideal customer which can be quite detailed. Some groups are so commonly used that they have their own acronyms: dual income no kids yet are 'Dinky's; young, executive and single are 'YES's; 'Yuppies' are young and upwardly mobile.

Some of the main methods of analyzing market conditions and positions are product portfolio analysis, perceptual analysis and SWOT analysis.

Product portfolio analysis looks at the range of products which a business sells. One tool used for product portfolio analysis is the Boston matrix (qv). The *perceptual map* of a product portfolio looks at the balance of products in terms of market coverage. A business may ask itself which market segment it is not currently targeting, but could.

Once a decision to widen a market base has been made, the Ansoff matrix (qv) can be used to show how safe or how risky various marketing objectives are. The market can also be analysed by conducting a SWOT analysis (qv).

All analyses and profiles are used to help inform marketing management decision making – it is the managers, rather than the techniques, who make the final judgement.

see also...

Ansoff matrix; Boston matrix; SWOT analysis;

Market research

Market research involves the collection, collation, analysis and interpretation of information regarding a particular market. It will involve both primary (field) and secondary (desk) research. *Primary research* is information that has not been collected before, it is 'first-hand' information. Often the methods of collecting primary research make it expensive, but it can be targeted and focused to collect exactly the information which the business needs. This may involve methods such as:

● observation
● interviews
● surveys – carried out amongst existing or potential customers
● questionnaires
● focus groups – small groups of people who are asked in-depth questions.

Often such research is disguised as something else: many competition entries ask for basic information about the entrant; guarantees will often only be validated by the purchaser filling in a guarantee card, again providing the business with vital information about its customers.

Secondary research is research that has been previously published. There are very good sources of secondary data such as government figures and statistics and numerous less-reliable sources. The problem with secondary research is that, while some of it may be cheap (it may even be free – many government collected statistics are available on the government web site at www.statistics.gov.uk) much of it will not fulfil the exact requirements of the business. Often secondary research may only provide background information.

see also...

Market segmentation; Market planning

Market segmentation

So that businesses can better target markets, they divide them up into smaller sections or segments. Each product can then have distribution, advertising, promotion, packaging and price tailored to a particular market segment. Some markets are segmented not once but many times, into smaller and smaller sub-sections. The smallest market segments are called *niche markets* and, while they may be a small segment of a market, they can still be very large in terms of numbers. For example, replica kit for a sports team might be considered a niche market, but could still run into many thousands of buyers.

The main ways in which markets are segmented are by age, gender and income. Each market segment can be targeted by advertising in particular ways or at particular times.

Targeting by age involves both distinct and different age groups and the spending patterns within those groups. Younger age groups have little spending power so advertisers rely on 'pester power' – making products so attractive to children that they will pester parents to buy them. Other important milestones are when couples are at their maximum earning potential, when they are likely to marry, when they have teenage children, when children have left home. Each group is given a tag to identify them to marketing managers (the last group, for example, are 'empty nesters').

Geographical targeting can take place by region, or even by postcode whilst targeting by income group (socio-economic group) is also important. Segments may also involve race and religion, habits, interests and hobbies.

The smallest market segment is a niche market of one – and some businesses target such a tiny segment by providing a personal service or by customizing products to an individual's requirements.

see also...

Socio-economic groups

Marketing constraints

These are limitations to what a business is allowed to do in its marketing. Constraints will either be internal constraints that are within the control of the business or external constraints that are outside its control. These include factors such as competitor reactions, the state of the economy and changes in legislation.

Government may limit or restrict the advertising of certain products (the television advertising of cigarettes or tobacco, for instance). Legislation may also be used to protect certain vulnerable groups – alcohol advertisements must not be aimed at teenagers, for example, and some products and services may only be sold under licence to certain age groups. Marketing law also protects consumers through the Trades Descriptions Act and various labelling and quality regulations.

Businesses usually prefer self-regulation to being told what they can and cannot do, and the advertising industry has its own independent watchdog bodies for both broadcast and print advertisements. The Advertising Standards Authority covers all print and published advertisements and has a Code of Practice which states that all advertising should be
● 'legal, decent, honest and truthful'
● 'prepared with a sense of responsibility to the consumer and society' and
● 'in line with the principles of fair competition'.

The Independent Television Commission (ITC) covers broadcast advertisements on television whilst the Radio Authority is the watchdog for radio.

Other external constraints include ethical, moral, environmental and social constraints.

Internal constraints may be lack of finance, lack of the appropriate personnel, or a particular company ethos or corporate image. These (particularly corporate) factors may be greater constraints than the external factors.

see also...
Consumer protection

Marketing mix

The marketing mix is the term given to the way that an entrepreneur sells a product. Successful sales (and therefore a successful business) depend on the product being offered at the right price, in the right place and with appropriate promotion methods. A marketing budget will be divided between these four areas of product, price, promotion and place.

The *product* refers to the goods or services that are produced by the business, the result of the combination of factors of production by the entrepreneur. A product may be either a (tangible) good or a (non-tangible) service and it is probably the most important part of the marketing mix. If the product is not good enough, no amount of promotion or pricing tactics will lead to its being successful.

Price is the second of the factors, it has to be set somewhere near the consumer's perceived value for the product. A consumer will have an idea of what a particular product should cost. Generally, this is governed by a factor called 'value for money'. If the business can charge the appropriate price – within the range of prices which a consumer considers value for money – sales will increase.

Promotion covers the various ways in which business brings its product to the notice of the potential consumer. This includes advertising, special offers, publicity stunts and other tactics.

Place covers both the premises where the product or the means by which it is offered for sale. It also includes distribution – the logistics of getting the product to the premises.

More important than allocating funds or efforts to each individual part of the mix is getting the balance right. The key to a successful product is a well-balanced marketing mix.

Price   Product

MIX

Promotion   Place

see also...

Price setting; Product; Distribution strategies; Promotion

Maslow's theory

Abraham Maslow was an American psychologist. He contended that workers only worked in order to gain certain needs but that these needs were hierarchical – the worker cannot attain the next need up the pyramid until s/he has attained the current one. Once a level is achieved, the worker then looks for the next level.

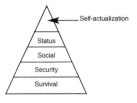

Firstly, the worker needs to satisfy *survival or subsistence needs* – in other words the worker needs the basics such as food and clothing. Secondly the worker will seek *security goals* – wanting to feel safe and clear of threat. Thirdly, once safety goals are met, people want to meet other people, they have social needs. Once this level is attained, the worker can look for higher order needs. The first of these is status – wanting to be respected and looked up to; the second is self-actualization or ambition fulfilled – the worker

finally attains everything that s/he has striven for.

In the context of a company, these needs might be seen as a decent wage, job security and a pension, team working, a title or other symbol of status and an achievement of some ultimate goal – perhaps a particular position within the company.

Maslow's theory laid the basis for much of the work of motivational theorists who followed him and his name is usually linked with McGregor and Herzberg. Other theorists have questioned the basis of the psychology. For example, is the goal of self-actualization ever reached? Is it true to say that everyone has the same needs? Are people happy to set short-term goals and only motivated to work towards them?

Questions such as these have been tackled by later theorists, but it was Maslow who laid the ground work.

see also...
Motivation theory; HRM

Motivation theory/theorists

With the advent of industrialization, managers began to look at ways of increasing the productive efficiency of their workers and at motivation. Early theorists were Henri Fayol (1841–1925), who developed the ideas of organization charts, spans of control and chains of command and Frederick W. Taylor (1856–1915), who concentrated on the efficiency of shop-floor workers rather than management. He developed what was called scientific management theory which said that it was management's job to organize workers efficiently and that the best form of motivation was more money. His theories were seen as influential and built on by many later theorists.

Elton Mayo (1880–1949), through his experiments in varying lighting conditions at the Hawthorne Electrical Factory from 1927 to 1932, decided that scientific management theory lacked a vital human element. His experiments showed that workers worked better if they were shown some attention and developed from this the Human Relations School of Management.

Abraham Maslow (1908–1970) theorized that workers had a hierarchy of needs that management should be trying to fulfil.

Frederick Herzberg (1923–1991) was an American psychologist who developed theories of job satisfaction including practical approaches such as job enrichment and job rotation.

Douglas McGregor (1906–1964) is best remembered for his proposal that workers can be grouped into two types (*The Human Side of Enterprise*, 1960) which he called Theory X and Theory Y. X workers are basically work shy, Y workers derive satisfaction from their work; different approaches to motivation are needed for the different groups.

Victor Vroom is a modern management writer who introduced the path–goal concept, otherwise known as expectancy theory. Motivation, he says, is linked to what the worker actually wants and how likely s/he thinks it is that they will get it.

see also...

Maslow's theory; Leadership styles

Mutual societies and demutualization

Mutual societies are a specialized form of co-operative enterprise. The two main groups of mutual societies are insurance companies and building societies. Some mutuals were established so that professional groups with excess cash could invest their money to provide a pension or income. These were linked to many of the wealthier professions, accounting for mutuals such as Legal and General and Clerical and Medical.

The principles of mutuality are that the business operates with the best interests of its members at heart. It is not therefore necessarily a profit maximizer, as the focus is on providing the best service at the best rates to members. It does not have shareholders to answer to, but a membership of borrowers and investors.

The deregulation of the financial services market has led to a number of mutual societies seeking to demutualize so that they can compete in the new markets. For example, building societies were allowed to operate current accounts and issue credit and debit cards and banks were allowed to issue mortgages. Some societies, such as Scottish Widows, Abbey National, Halifax and the Woolwich have demutualized, with cash or shareholding benefits going to members; others have resisted and remained as mutuals.

The process of demutualization is to change the mutual society into a public limited company by floating it on the Stock Exchange. The process of demutualization can be set in train by a single member of the mutual and usually involves the offer of shares in the new company or other financial compensation to members who will lose mutual benefits. It is the membership that have to decide whether or not to remain as a mutual, but in many cases, they have been persuaded by the prospect of a large windfall in cash or shares.

see also...

Co-operatives; Private business ownership

Operations management

Operations management is the term used to cover the co-ordination and control of the production process. It involves decisions regarding the scale, location and method of production to reach the optimum output along with considerations on how operations are to be controlled and inventory or stock control.

Initial decisions centre on what to produce, where, how and how many.

Deciding what to produce should be closely linked to market research findings. The location of business is decided on factors such as the proximity of raw materials or the state of the infrastructure. The scale of production can be decided by maximizing the economies of scale which the business can gain (and minimizing the diseconomies). Scale will be limited by the productive capacity of the business; this can be increased by adding more resources, increasing productivity (the relative efficiency of the factors of production) or by reorganizing the productive inputs (rationalization). Operations managers must also decide which production method will be the most efficient.

Networks, critical path analysis and Gantt charts are used in production control to show the manager what tasks need to be completed and when.

Good control of inventories (i.e. stock levels) can reduce a business's costs, so managers should try to keep the minimum of buffer stock levels (to cut down on storage costs) and lead-in times that are as short as possible (see figure).

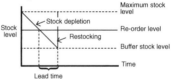

Control of production is now likely to involve lean production methods such as just-in-time production, where components arrive when they are needed, and cell production, where production is a function of teams rather than of a production line.

see also...

Cell production; Economies and diseconomies of scale; Lean production

Organization charts

Organization charts are used to show the structure and relationships within the organization of a business. For maximum efficiency, a business should choose the form of organization structure that best suits its size and its aims and objectives. In some organizations a formal and rigid structure is necessary (the army could not operate on an informal structure), in others – particularly the creative industries – it may be better to have less rigid structures.

Organization charts are typically shown as 'family tree' or T charts, circular charts or matrix structures. The figure shows a T chart being used to show a departmental structure, with some of the main roles and terminology of such a structure. A has authority over B, C and D, the departmental managers. Authority is the right to give orders or instructions to someone in the organization. A can also delegate authority to B, C and D, so that they can make decisions without referring to him. B, C and D are subordinate to A while E is subordinate to B. The *span of control* shows the number of subordinates over which someone has power, while the *chain of command* is the way in which instructions are passed through the various layers of the organization. In this case the chain goes from A to B to E. Taking out a layer of management (such as all those at B's level) would be called delayering. This is meant to make the structure more flexible. F has what is called a staff role; she reports directly to A and could have an advisory role, or be part of administration or accounts. B, C and D are line managers, with specific authority within the formal structure – part of the organization's hierarchy.

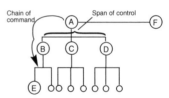

Organization charts are useful for showing the formal relationships between the various parts of an organization. However, in complex organizations – particularly where roles are multi-functional – they may not be clear enough to be of any use.

see also...
Management functions

Personalities

Business is often enlivened by a business personality, a man or woman who seems to stand larger than life on the business stage. Each generation seems to throw up its own particular favourites. The entrepreneurs may have a new 'big' idea; the organizers are likely to be building business empires. Current personalities include the following.

Rupert Murdoch is at the head of News International, the holding company for a vast media empire which is still acquiring more outlets and more market share.

Stelios Hajj-Ioannou is the latest in a long line of entrepreneurs who are trying to provide a cut-price service for air passengers. Hajj-Ioannou has launched EasyJet as an internet booking operation along with a string of other 'Easy-' type businesses and has sought a lot of publicity for his stand against the big airlines and for modern technology.

Anita and Gordon Roddick had a particular 'big idea' that caught the zeitgeist of the late twentieth century. They decided to source natural products, from unexploited workers, and present them in bottles that could be recycled to lessen pressure on the environment (and incidentally cut costs). Because of the environmental credentials of the company, Anita Roddick has always maintained a high profile.

Richard Branson likes to be thought of as the flamboyant head of a forward-looking company. Virgin started out with just one record store and has since expanded into travel, holidays, airlines, railways, insurance, mobile phones and more.

James Dyson is a different sort of business personality. An inventor who found his alternative system for vacuum cleaner technology being turned down by a well-established and complacent industry, he has since established a major presence in the market. He emphasizes the benefits of research and development.

see also...

Enterprise

PEST

Businesses are affected by a number of factors that are outside of their control. These are called external factors and traditionally include the four areas of political, economic, social and technological factors, called PEST. To these have been added environmental factors and legal factors so that the PEST acronym is no longer sufficient. Other versions now include SLEPT and STEEPLE.

Political factors include the constraints on the business brought about by the political colour of local, national and international governments.

Economic factors cover changes in consumer demand caused by alterations to income and expenditure patterns. These may be a result of changes in the business cycle or of macro-economic policies such as taxation or changes in interest rates.

Social factors are changes in consumer demand or business practice brought about by changes in society. Some will affect only a small proportion of businesses but may affect them in a big way.

Technological factors are changes in technology such as new materials, products or processes. For example, the internet has opened up many new business opportunities.

Legislation covers health and safety, employment rights and consumer rights. It affects all sections of the business community in regulating everything from standard weights and measures to the fire resistance of furniture and children's clothes.

Environmental factors have become increasingly important to businesses who want to be seen to have 'green' credentials.

A single change can often embody many external factors – if cannabis were legalized, for example, this would have legal, social, political and economic implications. It is not always easy, therefore, to separate factors out.

see also...

Government policies; Marketing constraints; EU policies

Peters, Tom

om Peters is probably the best known of current management experts. *In Search of Excellence*, written with co-author Robert Waterman and published by Harper and Row in 1982, is the best-selling business book in the world. The book looks at 43 top US companies, often household names, which had stayed in the top 50 per cent of their industries for 20 years or more. He used these companies to see if there were any common factors to their continuing success.

Peters and Waterman identified eight common factors. One of the major ones was to recognize that employees are an important part of the business and to treat them as valued assets. Employees were also valued for their ideas; any ideas or innovations that they come up with should be treated seriously and developed where possible.

Another factor was the use of small project teams to complete specific projects, often using matrix management techniques. These teams might also include a representative of the customer as a

further part of successful philosophy is that the business listens to customer concerns and acts on the feedback it receives. Businesses also showed an ability to concentrate on their core business, rather than diversifying into unknown territory.

Many of these factors have since been developed or denied by other theorists (and many of Peters' successful companies are no longer successful) but Peters' ability to put his point across has been his abiding strength. He addresses business meetings and seminars in an exciting and inclusive way and is said to motivate managers through his enthusiastic approach. He currently advocates flexible organizations which can change rapidly, and flexible employees. His code is one of inclusivity – everyone should be equally involved in the success of the business and equally able to contribute. The UK system of Investors in People (IIP) goes some way to encouraging this approach.

see also...

HRM; *Management theorists*

Price setting

Price is one of the elements of the marketing mix. The most common form of pricing is *cost plus pricing*. This is where the business adds up the various costs of producing the good or service – raw materials components, power, labour, etc. – and then adds on a percentage for profit (called a mark-up).

Businesses may link mark-up to the price that they feel a consumer will be willing to pay for the product. This is pricing made on the assumption that a consumer has a perceived value for a product – if the business can charge a price which reflects this value, then mark-up can be very high. (Think of a designer dress – what are the real costs of producing it in terms of materials and labour, yet what sort of price does it command?)

Most other methods of pricing can be called *competitive*, as they involve pricing in such a way that the good sells more than a competitor. Skimming and penetration prices are each pricing strategies that might be used when a new product is introduced onto the market. *Skimming* is used of products that can be sold at an initial high price. Often these are examples of new technology. *Penetration* pricing involves pricing at an initial low price in order to enter a market and build up a market share. Low prices may also be used in predatory pricing where a business deliberately undercuts rivals in an attempt to remove them from the market.

Some pricing strategies are more *promotional*. A loss leader is where a product is priced so low that it does not even cover its costs. This may be to attract buyers who will then realize the benefits of the product and continue to buy it; in retail terms it is usually a staple product (such as bread or milk) priced to attract customers into the shop so that they spend money (and therefore generate profits) on other products.

There are also pricing 'tricks' such as *psychological point pricing*. This is where prices are deliberately set below certain 'trigger' prices such as £5 or £100. Prices seem a lot lower when they are £4.99 or £99.99.

see also...

Marketing mix; Demand; Market failure

Private business ownership

The most popular and widespread form of business ownership is the *sole trader*, also called the sole proprietor or the one-man (or one-woman) business. Forty per cent of UK businesses registered for VAT are sole traders; there are huge numbers not registered for VAT. The sole trader is the easiest form of business ownership to set up and run. To set up, all the trader needs to do is to start trading. There are no necessary formalities (although the nature of the trading may be subject to permissions and regulations). The sole trader takes all the responsibility of running the business, takes all the decisions and, in return, takes all the profits. S/he also takes all the risk – this includes risking his/her personal wealth as s/he has unlimited liability for the debts of the business.

The next most common form of business ownership is the *partnership*. This is where a business is established and owned jointly by two or more people. This may be for a number of reasons. Partners may share the workload or a partner may bring a particular area of expertise to a business. Setting up a partnership is as easy as setting up as a sole trader but, because of the possibility of disagreements, partners are advised to draw up a partnership agreement. If they fail to do so then the Partnership Act 1890 comes into play, dividing everything equally. Usually profits and decision making are shared equally amongst the partners (although a partnership agreement can vary this). Partners each have unlimited liability, meaning that a partner with more assets could actually lose more if the business collapsed. Partners can limit their liability by being sleeping or silent partners – investing in the business but taking no part in running it.

Private limited companies are often family firms. The company has a separate identity from its owners, who benefit from limited liability, and sells shares. These shares are not publicly quoted nor for sale to the public.

> ### see also...
> *Co-operatives; Mutual societies and Demutualization; Franchises*

Privatization

This is where the government moves a business or organization from the public sector – owned or controlled by central or local government – to the private sector – owned by private individuals. The most common method, and the one that has come to epitomize privatization, is the selling of shares in businesses that were previously state owned. Major privatizations included gas, coal, electricity, the railways, water, steel and shipbuilding. These were made as part of a particular political philosophy which thought that private management would run such industries more efficiently than the public sector. Privatization, in many cases, was coupled with the idea that eventually competition would be introduced to replace state monopolies. It was believed that competition would provide lower prices, more choice and better allocation of resources. Some industries were also deregulated, allowing private companies to compete in areas where competition had previously not been allowed (bus services, for example).

At a local government level, councils were required to put services (such as refuse collection or school grounds maintenance) out to what was called 'competitive tendering'. This meant that private businesses could bid to run services. Again, this was meant to lead to better and cheaper services. Councils were also encouraged to sell off assets, such as council houses.

Further privatization has taken place through the Private Finance Initiative (PFI) and Public Private Partnerships (PPP). PFI means that, instead of government providing the finance for major capital projects, it is provided by private business.

PPP means that both public and private money is used for a project. Government and private sector finance share funding as a way of introducing private money and management into some public services. This is the scheme that has been proposed, controversially, both for the privatization of the London Underground and air traffic control.

see also...

Government Policies; Floating a company

Product

The product is what is actually produced as a result of business activity. It could be either a good or service. Goods are categorized as consumer durables, consumer non-durables and industrial goods. *Consumer durables* are those goods that can be used again and again – anything from a car to a toothbrush – even though they will eventually deteriorate. *Consumer non-durables* can only be used once – petrol or toothpaste, for example. *Industrial goods* are those that are going to be used as part of the production process such as factories, plant, equipment and tools. *Services* include personal services for individuals and groups or commercial services such as insurance, retailing and transport. Pop singers and professional sports people provide a service just as much as retailers or travel agents.

Consumers buy products to obtain both tangible and intangible benefits. Buying a branded sweatshirt may give the tangible benefit of keeping you warm and the intangible benefit of being seen to be fashionable. The intangible benefits, on many occasions, will outweigh the tangible ones. Products are usually bought for a combination of core reasons and peripheral reasons that are secondary to the core. The core reason for buying the sweatshirt may be to stay warm; the colour and style of the product will give secondary tangible benefits. The tertiary benefits will come from the promise of quality or acceptability provided by the brand. This is known as the augmented product.

Product range refers to the different product lines which a business sells, such as a range of snack foods. The product mix refers to the variety of product types. A narrow mix means that the business is dependent on a particular market segment and therefore vulnerable to changes.

Product differentiation is where businesses try to make their product different from those of their competitors. One of the major ways of achieving product differentiation is through branding.

> ### see also...
> *Marketing mix; Product life cycle*

Product life cycle

The product life cycle shows the usual stages through which a product passes from its original conception and development through to its eventual demise and withdrawal from sale. It is used as a planning tool by a business to show where development and promotion costs are likely to be highest, where sales and revenue can be expected to peak and where boosts to sales might be required. Managers can use it to change and develop promotion strategies.

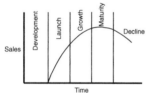

The typical product life cycle is shown here. Each segment does not represent a particular length of time as this will differ from product to product. Development can be a very long time period for some products and costs are high during this period. After the launch the growth period is characterized by increased sales and by competitors spotting the potential of the market and entering it with rival products. The *mature period* sees sales consolidated through promotional strategies and brand loyalty. Costs will begin to rise again as promotion is used to keep rivals at bay. Finally, the product declines – demand (or technology) moves on and the product is no longer needed and eventually withdrawn from sale. Successful products can have their life cycle extended through product extension strategies.

Some products suffer what are called aborted life cycles. Typically, a lot of money is spent on development and then the product fails to find a market.

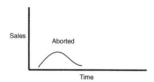

see also...

Product; Boston matrix; Market planning

Production methods

The process of production is also known as 'transformation'. It is the process by which raw materials and other inputs such as components are turned into outputs – at the end of the process these outputs are the final product. Production will be organized so that it takes place within safe limits, within a certain time span, and using chosen inputs such as machinery, labour and power. The method of production chosen by the entrepreneur will depend on the nature of the product and the nature of the customer. Services are almost always produced to individual standards for individual customers, for example, you can only wear your own haircut, not someone else's; a car service to a friend's car will not do your car any good! In the case of goods, some will be produced for a mass market, where the very fact that they are all identical is of benefit. The decision will have to be taken on which is the best method of production. Part of this decision will be whether production is capital or labour intensive. Capital intensive production involves more machinery than labour, whereas labour intensive involves more labour than machinery.

The main methods of production are job, batch, flow or mass and project.

Job production is where a product is a 'one-off' made to individual specifications, for example made-to-measure clothes. *Batch production* is where the same capital equipment and resources can be used to produce different batches or groups of products. For example, the same dress may be produced in sizes 8 to 16, the same car in different colours.

Flow production is also called *mass, continuous* or *process* production. This involves a product moving along a production line or being processed with modifications or additions made along the way.

Project production is where a one-off project, needing inputs from many different businesses and teams, is made. A good example could be the Millennium Stadium in Cardiff or a new road or bridge.

see also...
Lean production; TQM

Productive efficiency

If an organization can increase the productive efficiency of capital, or labour, then this is one way in which costs can be lowered. In terms of value analysis, greater productivity is a gain that should always be possible. Productivity is not, as is sometimes erroneously stated, a measure of how hard a person or machine works, what it measures is the efficiency of inputs and combinations of inputs in producing certain outputs.

Productivity is usually measured by looking at three particular inputs: labour, capital and materials (although the productivity of *any* input can be measured).

Labour productivity includes all labour inputs, not just manual but also non-manual and management inputs. The measurement would look at what the total capacity of labour was (how much could be produced if everyone worked at 100 per cent efficiency all of the time); how much of that total time was actually used, how productive labour was within that time (output per person, per hour, for example) and what the actual cost of labour was.

Capital productivity again would look at capacity and how much of it was being utilized; 'down time' (time out of service) for machinery for service and repair, the cost of operating machinery (such as power and expertise) and the original cost of buying the machinery. Output per machine, per hour is also included as a measurement.

Materials productivity is measured in terms of the original cost of the materials, how much wastage there is (and its value) and how much new product is created per amount of raw material input (the 'yield').

However, it is combinations of these measures which actually give the *total productivity* – or a better measure of efficiency – of the business. It is no use having a top quality machine that is being worked by someone untrained or inexperienced. An integrated approach to productivity measurement will therefore be more useful.

see also...

Factors of production

Profit

rofit is seen as perhaps the most important factor to a business. It is the reward to enterprise, or risk taking. Profit is defined as the difference between costs and revenues. For example, if you buy ten chocolate bars at £1 each and sell them for £1.10 each, your costs are £10, your revenue £11 and you have made £1 profit. Or have you? The important thing about calculating profits is to make sure that you take all costs into account. There may be obvious costs to the above transaction, such as driving to the shop, that have not been included; there may also be less obvious costs such as your own time, or the use of your own money to buy the chocolate. In a more complex business transaction (and most are a great deal more complex than this) it is easy to overestimate the amount of profit that has been made.

Profit is not just a reward, but also part of the signalling system of supply and demand. If profit is being made then this acts as a signal to other businesses to compete in a particular market. Losses are seen as a signal that there are too many businesses competing in a market.

Profit, in a company, may be undistributed or distributed. *Undistributed profit* is also called retained profit; it is the profit which the company keeps for itself in order to provide internal finance for improvements or expansion. *Distributed profit* is the amount divided amongst the shareholders to form their dividend. In a public limited company the amount of profit made and in particular the distributed profit will be important for keeping the shareholders happy. A company that can promise healthy profits and a good return on money spent on shares, will see its share price (and therefore value) rise.

The making of profit is considered by many to be the prima-facie case for going into business. Profit maximization (the making of as much profit as possible) is often cited as the central aim of businesses.

> *see also...*
> *Enterprise; Aims and objectives*

Profit and loss account

This shows the profit generated or losses made over a period of time. The profit and loss account is part of the essential accounts of a company, which must be produced to satisfy the requirements of the Companies Act along with the balance sheet and (for plcs) the cash flow statement. It consists of the Trading Account, the Profit and Loss Account and the Appropriation Account. The trading account shows the business's sales turnover as against the cost of buying materials, stock, etc., for sale (the

overheads and operational expenses for the year.

Overheads will include power, vehicle expenses, rates, wages, insurance, communication and administration. They also include depreciation, which may appear as a separate item on the accounts. Depreciation shows how a piece of capital equipment loses value over time merely through age or use.

The appropriation account shows what has happened to the net profit made by the company.

Item	Cost	Revenue	Totals
	£	£	£
Trading Account			
Turnover		10000	
Cost of sales	7500		
Gross profit			2500
Profit & Loss Account			
Gross profit			2500
Expenses	1000		
Operating profit			1500
Other revenue		1000	
Interest on borrowings	500		
Net profit			2000
Appropriation Account			
Net profit			2000
Tax	400		
Profit for distribution (earnings)			1600
Profit kept (retained profit)			1000
Dividends paid (distributed profit)			600

cost of sales). This gives a gross profit figure. The profit and loss account shows other income that the business might earn and all the other

see also...

Balance sheet; Cash flow forecast

Promotion

romotion is the methods that a business uses to communicate to consumers that their product exists and that it has features that will be of benefit to a consumer. Promotion first of all aims to make consumers (or potential consumers) aware of a product, through repetition it encourages them to remember the product and finally it tries to persuade them to buy it. A typical promotional campaign might start by generating interest in a product (without revealing any of the benefits), then describing what the product does, then trying to persuade consumers to buy the product.

The main way in which businesses carry out these aims is through advertising. Advertising is publicity for a product that is paid for directly; it is therefore called *above-the-line expenditure*. Advertising is used to promote products through broadcast and print media of various types. The main case in favour of advertising is that it informs – without it customers would not know what was on offer and would therefore not be able to make a choice. The case against advertising is that it is an unnecessary cost that is passed on to the consumer.

Below-the-line expenditure is promotion other than direct advertising. In promoting a product to a consumer, a business may use various techniques such as money off coupons, special offers, competitions, free samples and trials and loyalty cards. Products such as industrial goods may be promoted in different ways through, for example, trained salespeople who describe product benefits directly or through trade fairs and exhibitions.

Public relations is a term that can be used to cover any ways of generating publicity such as a stunt to gain publicity, a donation to a charity, or a press conference. Public relations is promotion that is designed to build a particular image in the minds of the consumer. Methods include sponsorship, endorsement and product placement. Many of these methods are successful in promoting products where advertising is not allowed, such as on the BBC.

see also...

AIDA; Branding; Marketing mix

Public sector

The public sector refers to those businesses and enterprises that are owned not by the public, but by local or national government on behalf of the public. Many of these are services that either could not be adequately funded by the private sector; are services where it is difficult to make economic charges (and therefore difficult to make a profit meaning no incentive for private sector businesses); or where other considerations such as national security are paramount.

With some major projects (such as the building of a new railway line, or of a bridge or the Channel Tunnel) capital investment needs to be made at the start of the project but any returns may take years to materialize. Often it is only governments that have the depth of resources needed for the levels of investment expenditure that are necessary. Such projects may be completely funded by government or, through Public Private Partnerships (PPP) and the Private Finance Initiative (PFI) may be a mixture of private and public sector investment.

Public goods are those for which it would not be possible to make an economic charge such as street lighting and roads; merit goods are those which governments felt that they ought to provide for social reasons, otherwise people will not make enough use of them. These include education and the health service.

National security and safety issues mean that the police and the fire services are publicly funded and the armed forces also remain under the direct control of the government. The National Health Service is funded largely through National Insurance contributions.

Some enterprises will have been nationalized, i.e. taken from private ownership into the public sector, while others will never have been in the private sector, having been established and funded by government from the first. This latter group includes organizations such as the BBC (set up with a charter).

see also...

Government policies;
Privatization; Market failure

Ratios, activity

inancial ratios are part of the 'tool kit' used by management to judge a business's performance. They are generated from financial accounts of the business and are one variable measured in terms of another (such as production to inputs).

The main users of ratio analysis are managers, investors and potential investors and other stakeholders such as suppliers, competitors and creditors.

The main activity ratios involve stocks, assets and borrowing. *Stock turnover* is calculated as cost of sales/stock – the higher the figure, the faster the stock turnover. *Asset turnover* is calculated as sales turnover/assets employed and measures how hard the assets of the company are working. Interest cover is how many times the operating profit can pay interest payments. In general a business would be looking for a ratio of between 3 and 4 (under 1 would mean it could not pay interest from profit).

Gearing is calculated as long-term borrowing/capital employed

expressed as a percentage. A high level of gearing means that a firm has a high percentage of borrowings and is therefore more vulnerable to adverse changes in the economy than a company with low gearing.

Liquidity ratios measure how capable a business is of paying its short-term liabilities. Current ratio or working capital ratio is measured as current assets/current liabilities. A healthy ratio would be in the region of 1.5:1 to 2:1. It measures how many times over the company could pay its current liabilities from its current assets. The acid test ratio is measured as current assets – stock/current liabilities. A healthy ratio is in the region of 0.8:1 to 1:1. This is the same measure as the current ratio except that the company's stock is not included as part of its assets; the assumption that stock will be sold is not made.

see also...

**Financial accounting;
Stakeholders; Balance sheet**

Ratios, profitability

Profitability or performance ratios measure the relationship between profit and other factors with shareholders' ratios as a special subset of these.

There are various measures of profit and therefore various profitability ratios. The *gross profit margin* is measured as gross profit/turnover and expressed as a percentage. A more accurate measure is the net profit margin, as this takes overheads into account. *Net profit margin* is measured as net profit/turnover and expressed as a percentage. The higher the percentage, the better the company is performing.

The most important profitability ratio is ROCE (Return On Capital Employed). It is calculated as operating profit/capital employed expressed as a percentage. It is often referred to as the primary efficiency ratio, underlining its importance in measuring performance. It shows the return that the business is getting on the long-term capital it is using. ROCE needs to be higher than returns that could be earned from safer investments.

Shareholder ratios are used by shareholders to assess the value of their investment against other companies and against other possible uses for their money (meaning that interest rates are again involved). The main ratios used are the return on equity, calculated as earnings/shareholders' funds and expressed as a percentage. This shows how much profit shareholders might expect compared to their investment – the higher the percentage, the better. *Earnings per share* is calculated as earnings/number of shares issued expressed in money terms. The *p/e ratio* is the price to earnings ratio, calculated as share price/profit available for distribution and measuring the value of the share against the dividends earned by the share. The p/e ratio is often quoted along with share prices.

Dividend yield is calculated as the dividend per share/price of share expressed as a percentage. The higher the figure, the better the return on the share. This return has links with ROCE, as it needs to be above that which could be obtained by no-risk investments.

see also...

Shares; Profit

Recruitment

Recruitment describes the process that a business goes through to make sure that it has the right number of workers of the calibre it needs. The recruitment process will usually be part of the duties of the human resources functional area. It will begin with a recognition that a certain job needs to be done, and that someone needs to be appointed. This may be as a result of expansion, changes in work practices, promotion or retirement.

A job analysis may be prepared, which is a detailed study of the job in terms of tasks to be carried out and the qualifications needed. The business will then be in a position to advertise for exactly the person it needs.

The job analysis is used as the basis for writing a job description. This is an outline of the main points regarding the job.

These two documents can then be used to write the person specification. This gives the characteristics and qualifications that the ideal candidate for the job will have. It is often divided into three areas: characteristics essential to the job (perhaps a qualification, skill or experience), desirable characteristics, and additional qualities that may be less tangible (such as a sense of humour, or the ability to work in a team). A detailed person specification will also show how each quality will be identified by the selection process – through references, letter of application, curriculum vitae (CV), interview or test, for example.

The actual selection process is then likely to involve most or all of the following stages: an initial enquiry, a letter of application or completion of an application form, the sending of a CV, and an interview. Selection will be on the basis of long listing (drawing up a list of those candidates who fulfil the essential requirements as identified in letters, forms or CVs) and short listing (selecting from the long list those applicants who will be interviewed). Sometimes a business identifies exactly who it wants for a job and 'head-hunts' them.

see also...

HRM; Employment contract; Employment law

Shamrock theory

This is a central theory of organization structure and culture developed by Professor Charles Handy. Handy has experience as an executive with BP Oil, an academic, a broadcaster with the BBC and a management writer. His major works are *Understanding Organizations* (Penguin, 1976) and *Inside Organizations* (BBC Books, 1990). The 'shamrock' organization of the future has three leaves to it (see figure). These are the core workers, the contract workers and the peripheral workers. He forecast that organizations would increasingly rely less on core workers and buy in expertise as and when they needed it.

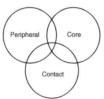

Core workers are professionally qualified and central to the business. They may be technicians, managers, engineers or other experts. They provide the strategic management for the business and a central reserve of expertise. They will be salaried and further tied into the business through pensions.

Contract workers will be employed for a fixed duration, either a time period or for the completion of a project. They will not be party to the organizational benefits of the company such as pensions.

Peripheral workers are employed on a part-time or short term basis as and when they are needed. They may be self-employed freelance workers or supplied by an agency. The use of such workers means that the business can be flexible – having more staff when it needs them but not having to pay them at other times. Flexible working is in contrast with the traditional paternalistic bureaucratic organization and means much more training and retraining.

A worker should now expect to retrain and do many different jobs during his or her working life rather than the old 'job for life' philosophy.

see also...

Management theorists; HRM

Shares

A share is initially issued to a shareholder in return for a payment to a company. It gives a share in the value of the company, in the decision making of the company and in the profits of the company. Shares may also be termed stocks, equities or securities. They also come in different varieties according to what order they are repaid should the business go into liquidation, or according to their voting strength. The most common are termed *ordinary shares*.

One method of estimating the value of a company is to multiply the price of the share by the number of shares issued. This is why, when the price of a share falls on the Stock Exchange, it may be reported that 'millions have been lost from the value of such-and-such a company'. (The company, however, still has the same equipment, products, staff and order books as it had the day before so it can be seen that there are other ways by which value might be measured.) The decision making is through having one vote per ordinary share at the Annual General Meeting (AGM) of the company, which can be used to elect directors or to agree or disagree with company policy. Of course, anyone with enough shares will have a controlling interest and can make whatever decisions they want. The share of profits comes through the dividend paid to shares. This is the profit which the business does not retain, but divides equally between each share.

It is the demand and supply of shares on stock markets that determine the value of them. The company issuing ordinary shares does not intend to redeem them, but owners can sell them to anyone who wants them (shares are sometimes referred to as 'second hand' for this reason). When prices are generally rising, this is called a *bull market*; when prices are generally falling, it is called a *bear market*. The rise and fall of the stock market is often seen as an indicator of the general health or otherwise of the economy. A bull market is meant to indicate a healthy business sector, a bear market a troubled one.

see also...

Profitability ratios; Floating a company

Small businesses

The majority of businesses in the UK can be classified as small, with many of them being either sole traders or small partnerships. Four out of every ten businesses registered for VAT are sole traders. Bearing in mind that a certain turnover threshold has to be reached before registration is compulsory, it is not surprising to find that two-thirds of all businesses in the UK are sole traders. In fact, out of the 3.7 million businesses in the UK, 99.2 per cent were defined as small. But what is a small business? The Bolton Committee, in 1971, set out to define 'small' and decided that it meant a small share of the market along with independent and personal management (i.e. owner/managers such as sole traders and partnerships). Other definitions include a turnover of less than £2 million, 50 employees or less and assets of under £1 million.

When there are so many apparent advantages from the economies of scale that can be gained through growth, why do so many businesses remain small? The main reason is that the owners want them to stay small. Not every business owner is ambitious to expand and run a multi-national corporation. Many of the objectives of the owners of small businesses are satisficing ones. There may also be a fear that, if the business grows any bigger, they might lose their independent control. The bigger the business is, the harder it will be to maintain the hands-on management style typical of small business owners.

With some businesses it may be impractical to expand. Many small businesses involve craft and other skills where it would not be possible to develop a mass market approach. Other businesses may provide a customised service. Some types of service may also be more efficient if kept to a local area – a pizza seller would not be willing to deliver outside a certain radius, for example.

Many small businesses are catering to a niche market. Whilst this means that they will have guaranteed custom and probably little competition, there will be no room for expansion.

see also...

Break even; Costs; Economies and diseconomies of scale; Private business ownership

Socio-economic groups

This is one of the main ways of dividing a market to identify a particular market segment. The market is divided according to the occupation and income of the head of the household. This is not completely accurate, but gives a very good general picture to those wishing to target a particular market segment. Information is collected and collated nationally, through the National Census which takes place every ten years, and through various other large-scale surveys. Research can be used to show different variables, the main ones being socio-economic, demographic (relating to population), ethnographic (relating to ethnic origin), geographic and psycho-graphic (relating to behaviour and habits) and combinations of these.

There are five main socio-economic groups. Group A are classified as 'professional' and include top civil servants, judges, hospital consultants, top engineers and architects. They comprise only 3 per cent of the population but have enormous spending power. Group B is 'professional, managerial and executive'; this group includes bank managers, university lecturers, senior managers in industry, solicitors, engineers, and barristers. They are just 12 per cent of the population. Although Groups A and B represent only 15 per cent of the population, they carry almost all of the potential expenditure on luxury goods. Group C is so large that it is generally split into two groups: C1 and C2. C1 is 'supervisory and clerical' staff and includes sales assistants, junior managers and administrative jobs; C2 is 'skilled manual' workers such as carpenters, plasterers, plumbers, mechanics and electricians. This group represents over half of the population, 20 per cent in C1 and 33 per cent in C2. Group D is 'semi-skilled workers' such as fitters, packers and assembly line workers. This represents 20 per cent of the population. Group E is 'unskilled manual' workers such as cleaners and labourers. This group also includes anyone else on a low income such as the unemployed, students and people on state pensions.

see also...

Branding; Market segmentation; Market planning

Sources of finance

For many small businesses the major form of finance will be the owner's own funds. These may also include the profits of the business being re-invested. Other funds will be borrowed.

Short-term loans are usually measured in terms of months, but may still be considered short term to a maximum of three years. They may be obtained from bank overdrafts or loans or through various forms of credit.

Credit may come through the trade, through using credit cards or through buying machinery, vehicles, tools or other capital equipment on hire purchase. Stock is often bought on credit, the trader hoping to have sold the stock before it must be paid for. Credit cards may be used by a small trader to give a permanent and flexible source of extra funds.

Medium-term finance is generally accepted as finance taken out over a period of three to ten years. Finance will be obtained through medium-term loans which are likely to be used to buy fixed assets.

Long-term finance, loans from ten years upwards, may be obtained through banks specialising in commercial loans or through mortgaging land or property.

Personal loans may also be made by investors willing to supply venture capital. Such individuals are often known as business 'angels'.

Finance may also be raised through government grant or related schemes. The government has a number of schemes in place which are designed to help small businesses. The Business Start Up Scheme is designed to help the long-term unemployed to get back to work by setting up their own business. The Small Firms Merit Award for Research and Technology (SMART Award) is intended to give financial help to small firms at the 'cutting edge' of new technology and The Princes Trust provides grants and other assistance to young people under the age of 30 wanting to set up in business.

> ### see also...
>
> *Balance sheet; Cash flow forecast; Profit and loss account; Profit*

Stakeholders

The idea of the stakeholder is a fairly recent one to business. It was coined by American management writer Igor Ansoff in 1965 and is meant to show that there are many other groups, not just the owners, who have a stake, or interest, in business. Stakeholders include the customers of the business, its managers, its employees, its suppliers, its competitors and the community in which it operates. This means that the business has a set of obligations to all of these groups, not just to its owners.

The problem with recognizing the existence and importance of stakeholders is that there are likely to be conflicts of interest between different stakeholder groups.

When conflicts between stakeholders arise, this can be very damaging to a business. There are therefore mechanisms already in place to try either to make sure such conflicts don't arise, or to solve them if they do. The major conflict in many companies is often between shareholders, who want profits for the business converted into dividends for themselves, and customers, who want good service and fair prices.

Since the stakeholder concept has taken root, there has been a debate as to whether companies should consider their primary responsibility as being to shareholders or stakeholders. The Hampel Report in 1997 was set up to look into the way in which businesses operated, and was expected to tackle issues such as excessive directors' pay and responsibilities to stakeholders other than shareholders. The report was greeted with some disappointment when it recommended that the *status quo* remain. This conclusion did not surprise some commentators as the committee chairman, Sir Ronnie Hampel, was chairman of ICI and over half the committee was drawn from large corporations.

see also...

Shares

Statistics

tatistics provide important information to businesses. Statistical terms include:

- The mean, or 'average' response.
- The median, or central point.
- The mode, or most commonly occurring.
- Standard deviation, which shows the distribution of responses around the mean value.

The higher the standard deviation, the greater the dispersal of results; the lower the deviation, the more concentrated the results.

Imagine that you run a restaurant which has ten meals on the menu. For each meal (1 to 10), the number of servings you have sold in the previous week was:

1	2	3	4	5	6	7	8	9	10
4	7	7	8	6	4	5	3	2	4

The mean number sold (the average) is the total divided by the number of responses 50/10 = 5. The average number of servings is 5. The median divides the data into a top half and a bottom half – putting the responses in order gives 2 3 4 4 4 5 6 7 7 8. The median is the central figure, in this case, with ten responses, the fifth – 4.

This means that half the meals sell more than four servings, half sell four or less. The mode is the most commonly occurring figure, again in this case 4. This is important for businesses that deal in different sizes or styles – how many red cars, for example. In this case, if the restaurant keeps a stock of four of everything, it has a better chance of satisfying most customers. With a stock of four of each variety, 13 customers are unsatisfied and just three meals are wasted.

Statisticians have other ways of interpreting statistics to provide useful information. The problem with statistics is that they can be manipulated too much and sometimes serve to obscure information rather than reveal it.

see also...

Forecasting

SWOT analysis

SWOT analysis is one of the ways that a business can analyse its position in the market or markets where it sells its products. SWOT stands for the Strengths and Weaknesses, Opportunities and Threats which the business can perceive. Strengths and weaknesses are considered to be internal, i.e. within the control of the business, whereas opportunities and threats are considered to be external, i.e. outside the control of the business. Businesses can gauge the importance of each of these factors and work out how to minimize the negative ones and take advantage of the positive ones by carrying out an internal audit.

Internal strengths may include particular product lines, or strong product recognition through branding. They may also include less tangible factors such as the experience of staff, or the good relations between workers and management.

Internal weaknesses may be poorly performing products, weaknesses in structure or organization or poor communications. Internal weaknesses are not only difficult to detect, but often even harder to accept or to do something about. Whilst the definition of an internal problem means that it is within the control of the business (not necessarily 'within' the business – it could, for instance be a problem with a supplier) this often makes them harder problems to deal with.

External opportunities that may be presented include changes in the market, good publicity and changes in legislation. They may also include less concrete opportunities such as changes in trends, that a business will need to spot. *External threats* can come from many sources; it may be possible to predict some of them, such as a competitor entering a particular market, or government-led tax changes in a budget, while others will be completely unexpected. The more flexible the business is, the better its response to such threats is likely to be. Often the 'threats' are referred to as 'challenges' to make them sound more positive.

> ### see also...
> **Market planning; Boston matrix**

Total Quality Management

Total Quality Management (TQM) is a concept developed by the Japanese for, initially, the more efficient production of cars. It is not a single action, but one that is made up of a number of different facets, meaning that quality is the responsibility of everyone in the organization.

Edward Deming (1900–1993), known as the 'father' of TQM, introduced his ideas to the Japanese in 1950. This was that quality was more important than any other aspect of production. He outlined the system in 14 management points including:

● There should be continual improvement in the workplace.
● There should be a 'right first time' culture to reduce the need for quality inspection.
● Use modern methods of HRM, including training techniques, for management at all levels.
● The leader's or manager's role is to enable others to do their job better.
● Efficient two-way communication is essential.
● The barriers between line and staff employees should be broken down.
● Appraisal systems and management by objectives should not be used as they undermine the pride of employees in their own work.
● Employees should be encouraged to improve themselves through a process of continuous education.

Two main aspects of TQM are zero faults and quality circles. *Zero faults* is part of Deming's 14 points and is a system where there is 'zero tolerance' to faults; in other words, the standard should be perfection. Employees are rewarded with extra payments – often part of the savings that have been made – for ensuring that products are perfect from start to finish.

Quality circles were developed first by Toyota as an extension of TQM and team working. Groups of employees meet in the business's time to discuss and resolve quality issues, with the viewpoints of management, design, production and customer represented.

see also...

Japanese methodologies; Lean production; HRM; Cell production

Trade or business cycle

The trade cycle is also referred to as the business cycle. It is the cycle through which the economy is said to move during each nine- to ten-year period. It charts recession and recovery in the economy and may also be referred to as the cycle of 'boom and bust'. Governments have recognized the importance of these cyclical fluctuations to business and have tried to 'iron out' the ups and downs.

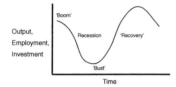

At the top of the cycle, the economy is said to be 'booming'. There is high demand but businesses are finding it impossible to increase supply to match it. As full employment is neared, wage rates rise and subsequently so do prices. Interest rates may also be high. Indicators show that the economy is overheating and people's expectations are that recession will follow. Business expectations tend to be self-fulfilling.

During a recession, demand falls meaning that businesses see an increase in stock. The fall in demand and excess supply means that prices are either stable or decreasing. Employment falls as businesses no longer need to increase production, but need to cut back. The pressure on interest rates will be for them to increase, causing further reductions in demand and increased business costs.

As the cycle 'bottoms out' with low demand and high interest rates, businesses will also have used up all of their stock. Expectations will be that things can 'only get better' so businesses start to invest in new stock. Financial institutions may find that they have a surplus of cash and no one willing to borrow it.

As the economy moves into recovery extra employment is created, demand increases and interest rates fall. This encourages increased investment as well as increased consumer expenditure.

see also...

Government policies

Variances

Variances are the differences between the budgeted or forecast level of a business's costs and revenues and the actual levels. They are a part of management accounting in a business.

Variances are either positive or negative. This means that they are either doing better than predicted or worse. The 'positive' and 'negative' tags can cause some confusion, as a minus variance may actually be positive. For example, if a predicted cost was £100 and actual cost was £90, then the variance would be −£10; however, because this is favourable, it is a positive variance.

Variances are usually calculated on the costs of materials and labour as these are the inputs which cost the most; variances can also be calculated, however, on any input for which there is a standard price. Material variances can be either price variances or usage variances. A material *price variance* is the difference between the standard (expected) price and the real price. *Usage variance* (the difference between the predicted and actual amount of materials used) may be due to the quality of materials, the efficiency of other inputs such as labour or the amount of wastage that occurs.

Labour variances are linked to either the price of labour or to its efficiency. *Labour price variances* can be caused by pay awards, by using labour that is better or worse qualified than planned (and therefore more expensive or cheaper) or by the imposition of a minimum wage.

Productivity variances (linked to the levels of efficiency of labour) can be due to the levels of training from which workers have benefited to the working methods adopted by the business and to levels of motivation within the business.

The value of variance analysis lies in managers being able to isolate where increased costs are actually occurring and take remedial action in that specific area.

see also...

Forecasting; Statistics; Cost and profit centres

World Trade Organization

The World Trade Organization (WTO) is the successor to the General Agreement on Tariffs and Trade (GATT). It is an international organization that is dedicated to freeing up international trade, i.e. to the removal of tariff barriers, quotas, embargoes and other restrictions on trading between nations. There have been several 'rounds' of talks to reduce tariffs, all lasting several years. The Kennedy Round ran from 1962 to 1967 and achieved a 35 per cent reduction in tariffs round the world. The Tokyo Round ran from 1973 to 1979, and the Uruguay Round from 1988 to 1994. The Uruguay Round set up the WTO as a replacement for GATT in 1995.

The WTO has become a target for protest groups as its negotiations are seen by many as encouraging both the growth of business and trade to the detriment of the environment, and the liberalization of trade to the detriment of the less-developed nations. For example, a suggestion made in 1996 that countries with cheap labour should adopt western labour practices such as minimum wages and working hours caused problems. Developing nations see low wage, for example, as the only way in which they can compete with their more developed neighbours. Free trade would effectively mean that they could no longer undercut the labour prices of the developed nations.

To businesses, freer world trade might mean easier access to world markets or, conversely, that competitor businesses have easier access to markets. The WTO is criticized for becoming more and more a tool of multi-national enterprises and a symbol of all that is wrong with globalization. Many multi-nationals quietly take advantage of cheap and non-union labour to keep production costs down, while many developing countries in the so-called Third World are saddled with enormous debt repayments from aid packages given by industrialized nations. Because the interest payments on this debt have become so high, it is increasingly difficult for them to trade on an equal footing with richer countries.

see also...

Globalization; Government policies

Index